Starting
a Business
in France

UN PETIT PIECE D'ANGLETERRE

Starting

a Business

in France

A STEP-BY-STEP GUIDE

RICHARD WHITING

howtobooks

Published by How To Books Ltd
Spring Hill House, Spring Hill Road
Begbroke, Oxford OX5 1RX
Tel: (01865) 375794. Fax: (01865) 379162
email: info@howtobooks.co.uk
www.howtobooks.co.uk

ISBN 10: 1 84528 123 3
ISBN 13: 978 1 84528 123 6

British Library Cataloguing in Publication Data
A catalogue record for this book is available from the British
Library

The right of Richard Whiting, to be identified as the author of this
work has been asserted by him in accordance with the
Copyright, Design and Patents Act 1988

Cover design by Baseline Arts Ltd, Oxford
Produced for How to Books by Deer Park Productions,
Tavistock
Typeset by Pantek Arts Ltd, Maidstone, Kent
Printed and bound by Cromwell Press Ltd, Trowbridge, Wiltshire

NOTE: The material contained in this book is set out in good
faith for general guidance and no liability can be accepted for
loss or expense incurred as a result of relying in particular
circumstances on statements made in this book. Laws and
regulations may be complex and liable to change, and readers
should check the current position with the relevant
authorities before making personal arrangements.

Contents

Preface

200,000 businesses on average are started every year in France and approximately 50 per cent of them fail or change their proprietor or legal status during the critical first five years. The failure rate is a high proportion of this percentage. Motivation is certainly not lacking as 300,000 salaried positions annually in the job market are not filled. Choosing to work for yourself, rather than having to, is the main motivation. *INSEE* (the national institute for statistics and economic research) reveals that almost 60 per cent of unemployed people who start their own business already had this in mind when they were still in salaried employment. Around a third of new businesses are created by the unemployed.

Getting market research, finance, advice, short- and medium-term business development plans, administrative details and suitable initial legal structure for the business right are essential. All these elements are or can be different in France. The first part of this book covers these themes. Despite the easier administrative path created by Dutreuil's law in 2003, starting a business in France certainly remains more difficult than in the UK. The capitalist economy is still heavily influenced and regulated by the state. English-speaking entrepreneurs with previous experience of starting and running a business in more liberal markets relatively free from state controls may find the French system frustrating. But they will have the risk-taking edge over French entrepreneurs starting up for the first time and who have no business experience outside of France. Anglophones moving to France to start a business are more adaptable, and more prepared to do something completely different than their French counterparts moving to the UK. Motivations are not the same. France's way of life is the real attraction for Anglophones, not money. While the UK's attractions for high-flying young French executives are better career and financial prospects. Different professional, commercial and customer attitudes, a different language and a different accounting system (unless your business graduates to the stock market where the International Accounting Standards Board system – mainly based on the American and British systems – is *de rigueur*) will need to be understood. Nationals from all European Union countries and Monaco are automatically entitled, provided they have elected residence in France or qualify for residence in Monaco, to start a business in France. The French residence card (*carte de séjour*) for EU members issued by the *service administration Etrangers* office of the national police confirms this entitlement '*toutes activités professionnelles en vertu du règlement 1612.68*'.

Equally important, especially for people who have never run their own business before, is organising their personal life for optimum family support, especially in the early start-up period, and protecting their personal estate against liability if the enterprise fails. Not everyone, even with the best advice money can buy and the best idea on the market, has the all-round qualities required to be a successful businessperson.

This book not only covers how to start a business, but also deals with the all-important prior questions of why, what, where and when. These four questions all require satisfactory answers before deciding to take the first practical step, a detailed market research report, when recourse to employing professional researchers may be appropriate. The three chapters in the second part of the book look at day-to-day basics to ensure the business' survival: organising and maintaining the accounts correctly, creating time to plan and see through the development of the business, keeping customers and attracting new ones, and taking on staff.

Reference is made throughout to private and state organisations and associations to contact for low-interest-rate loans, business development awards and advice (which is sometimes offered free from working or retired company directors). Some associations and organisations are national and others only exist in certain regions or *départements*. As well as immediate reference to relevant websites in the text a selection of appropriate websites is sometimes included at the end of each topic or chapter.

Taking the time to read *Starting a Business in France* will not guarantee success, but it will give step-by-step guidelines and useful tips which will help you avoid making any disastrous decisions and save time and money. The book is designed so that key information can be quickly and easily referenced.

Richard Whiting

Acknowledgements

I would particularly like to thank Sarah and Ian Smith of *The Connexion* newspaper, Nicholas Hill of Real Land and Adrian Byrnes of Charpentiers Réunis Mediterranée who told me how they started their businesses, and also Pierre Bernois of DTZ Jean Thouard and Madame Barthel of the Centre d'Affaires des Playes who helped me with information for the chapter on Premises.

TAKE MORE OF YOUR MONEY WITH YOU – WITH CURRENCIES DIRECT

If you're starting a business in France it's likely that the last thing on your mind is foreign exchange. However, exchange rates are constantly moving and as a result can have a big impact on the amount of money you have to start your new life in France.

For example, if you look at the euro during 2005 you can see how this movement can affect your capital. Sterling against the euro was as high as 1.5124 and as low as 1.4086. This meant that if you had £200,000 you could have ended up with as much as €302,480 or as little as €281,720, a difference of over €20,000.

To ensure you get the most for you money it's a good idea to use a foreign exchange specialist. As an alternative to your bank, a specialist is able to offer you extremely competitive exchange rates, no commission charges and lower (if any) transfer fees. This can mean considerable savings on your transfer when compared to using a bank.

Buying Options

Spot Deal – This is the *Buy now, Pay now* option and will give you the best rate available right now and guarantee it.

Forward Contract – This is the *Buy now, Pay later* option and allows you to fix a rate for anywhere up to 2 years in advance.

Limit Order – You set the rate that you want and the market is then monitored. As soon as that rate is achieved the currency is purchased for you.

Information provided by Currencies Direct.
www.currenciesdirect.com Tel: 0845 389 1729
Email: info@currenciesdirect.com

PART 1

Setting Up the Business

(1)

All-important prior questions

WHY START A BUSINESS IN FRANCE?

There may be several motivations for deciding to set up a business in France. Extra income to supplement pension, a completely new start with a planned permanent move to France, the satisfaction of being your own boss after redundancy or following a lifetime of salaried employment in France or elsewhere – or both – or, more rarely, the start of a working life following a period of apprenticeship or higher education.

Whatever the reason – with the possible exception of topping-up pensions where limited revenue is allowed on an occasional service-provider basis (prestataire de service occasionnelle) – such as letting rooms for under 13 weeks a year without having to establish an official business – success will require full-time commitment. Working harder and longer hours than before is to be expected, especially for non-French-speaking people arriving in France who have always previously been employees. The business will become a way of life, certainly in the early years. Separating 'living' from 'working' in France will be difficult. Apart from driving motivation and getting the project's choice right, bags of endurance (things often go wrong before they go right), patience (setting-up procedures and approvals can be complicated and take time) and style (appreciated by the French market) all help. Despite having advice and support available from family, a business partner, if you have one, and your professional advisors, be prepared to handle all conceivable problems which may just occur at the same time. The odds are they won't, but there will be days 'like that'! The buck stops with you and will be more difficult to stop in a foreign environment.

Think through the evolution of the project from conception, operation and development to long-term resale possibilities. A chart in Appendix 3 shows approximate resale values for different businesses (évaluation du fonds de commerce). Could family environment and personal health suffer? What personal financial resources can be risked, and written off at worst? Do you want to stay a small one-man band, keeping administrative paperwork down to a bare minimum and never have to change your business' legal form (forme juridique)? (See Chapter 3 and consider which forme juridique will best suit your project and protect your estate.) Or are you an expansionist, planning to take on staff to help the business grow? While growth may not be a priority, adaptability and the ability to introduce new products or modify existing ones will be necessary for survival in a perpetually changing marketplace. (Even Marks and Spencer cut their losses and withdrew from France in 2001 as they were not prepared to invest in the changes demanded by the French market.)

WHAT SORT OF BUSINESS DO YOU WANT TO START?

The nature of the business is as important as motivation. A gap in a well-known market will be easier and require less investment to tap successfully than the launch of an unknown, albeit innovative – perhaps revolutionary – product or service. Previous related experience in a particular activity is obviously better than a complete change in direction. Draw up three lists, A, B and C. List A should contain what you know how to do, List B what you would like to do and List C the market or potential market you feel exists for products or services for Lists A and B. If there is an area common to Lists A, B and C it would be sensible to investigate it in detail as the basis for the business project.

France's consumers are, ethnically, a rich, colourful mix with exotic and more European tastes, particularly in the fields of shops selling food, furniture, soft furnishings and soft goods, which are all widely catered for. There is scope here for new businesses.

An Ifop survey in January 2005 showed that 70 per cent of all new entrepreneurs were men with an average age of 39 and with, in the great majority, considerable management experience following at least a successful baccaluréat (which is roughly equivalent to GCSE Advanced Level) level of education: they are known as mid-way career men. Women are confirmed as being particularly good at running shops. The same Ifop survey indicated that 25 per cent of adults they interviewed would like to create their own business: just marginally below the UK figure of 28 per cent.

Franchises should not be overlooked, although considerable investment in successful brands and expertise will be required. McDonald's, for example, have never looked back since they opened in France about 20 years ago and Quick, their European competitor, continue to trade successfully in the 'fast-food' hamburger and salad market alongside them.

About 80 per cent of all new businesses are in the service and commercial sectors. Private training and educational establishments (which include EFL (English as a Foreign Language) teaching schools) and home-help businesses (gardening, meals-on-wheels, cleaning etc.) are particular segments where new business registration shows a marked increase. Geographically, the Limousin region, which is becoming extremely popular with British homeowners, shows an increase of slightly over 10 per cent annually in all types of new businesses which is far ahead of other regions.

Practice in the medical, legal and accountancy professions requires a state-recognised diploma. Building, electronic, mechanical and technical fields demand practical experience following formal training to be competent. Many trades and other professions have strict working regulations or demand a minimum number of years previous experience in a similar or identical activity before a new business can be authorised by their ruling bodies which then issue a working licence (carte professionnelle). Some of those businesses most likely to interest foreigners are: modelling agency (agence de mannequin); estate agent (agent immobilier), although no special qualifications are required for property search agencies; antique dealer (antiquaire); camp-site operator (gérant de camping); bars selling alcohol; shops selling cigarettes; hotels; restaurants; landscape gardeners (paysagistes) and child care centres (garderies d'enfants). Details for all trades and businesses can be obtained from the local CFE (Centre de Formalités d'Entreprises) department, depending upon activity, of the trade guild (Chambre des métiers), Chamber of Commerce and Industry, Agricultural guild (Chambre d'agriculture), or *URSSAF* (social security contributions collection agency) office.

Different procedures, not necessarily qualifying regulations, may also apply in France. National federations will usually be prepared to supply information, often free of charge, on their trades whether the enquiry is to supplement or confirm information for people with previous experience in their field or to provide information packages for complete newcomers. Membership of a federation will be invaluable later on in terms of marketing a new business and creating customer confidence.

Consult the ROME (Répertoire Opérationnel des Métiers et des Emplois) information sheets as well, on the national employment agency website www.anpe.fr or visit an ANPE office. These sheets (fiches) detail what specific trades, professions and service activities demand in terms of usual work tasks and conditions, required or recommended qualifications, ideal experience and personal aptitudes and qualities. They also indicate other activities which are similar or have some common ground with the particular activity being consulted. This is also invaluable for composing employment advertisements if you decide later on to employ people.

If you do plan to launch a completely new product, process or design, patent it (déposer le brevet) in your name as inventor or in the name of the company (see the What name? section on p73) at the Institut national de la propriété industrielle (INPI), 26 bis, rue de St-Petersbourg, 75008 Paris Cedex 08. There are also regional offices for the INPI in Bordeaux, Grenoble, Lille, Lyon, Marseille, Nancy, Nantes, Nice, Rennes, Strasbourg and Toulouse. An international agreement with most countries in the world gives the patent holder the possibility of protecting his patent on an international scale in the first 12 months following its issue. Details of this, current registration fees and periods of validity can be obtained from all the *INPI* offices. Patents are issued for all inventions considered to provide a technical solution to a technical problem. They must have an industrial application which implies a completely new type of business activity. Just because your 'baby' is going to look much nicer than what is on the market is not a valid reason for delivery of a patent. Although new computer programs cannot be patented with the *INPI*, the *Agence pour la protection des programmes* (*APP*) at 119, avenue de Flandre, 75019 Paris, assists or mediates in copyright disputes and will record the first publication (fabrication) date of new programs. Bear in mind that some patents have never been exploited commercially, but they may just decide to come onto the market as you plan to go into business.

While innovation is to be congratulated, guest-houses, camping and caravan sites, building and estate agency services remain amongst the most popular businesses with foreigners.

Guest-houses

Guest-houses include both *gîtes* and *chambres d'hôtes*. Basically, the *gîte* classification means self-catering rural accommodation. The national federation, *Gîtes de france* (www.gites-de-france.fr) is the largest federation for this type of accommodation in the world so application to become a member should not be ignored although at least 12 per cent of annual receipts must be paid to remain a member. Check out any particular rules the federation lays down regarding types of property as this may have a direct bearing on the property which is intended to be used.

Chambres d'hôtes (paying guest rooms) are the bed and breakfast accommodation market. British clientele may be happy with a continental – coffee and croissant – breakfast which must be substantial, but expect a semi-gastronomic evening meal as part of the accommodation package, while French clientele will look forward to the famous traditional English breakfast, if they know you're British, and be prepared to dine elsewhere in the evening. Offering a compromise between both meals is a good solution to attract all European nationalities. More than five rooms automatically up-grades an establishment to one star hotel status which means that rooms must be large enough for at least one chair for each occupant with one in five possessing an *en suite* bathroom and WC.

Camping and caravanning sites

Although the attraction of not accommodating people in your own home may appeal, camping and caravanning sites have a limited season and can involve considerable investment in essential facilities and services such as toilets, washrooms, showers and outdoor lighting. An all-year round complementary activity which involves little effort after the strict tempo of the camping season, such as renting space for open-air garaging of pleasure boats, may be necessary.

Official planning permission is required to create more than six individual camping/caravanning spaces. The overall plot of land set aside for this purpose must be level and cover at least 1,050 m^2, i.e., at least 150 m^2 per tent or caravan including their share of the facilities. A minimum plot of around two acres (8,000 m^2 is recommended to accommodate sufficient campers to make the business pay.

Builders

All professional builders must have insurance to provide the necessary two and/or 10-year construction guarantee cover for their work. The two-year guarantee (*garantie biennale*) covers all items such as taps, boilers, blinds, doors and electrical equipment which can be removed without damaging the building structurally. The 10-year guarantee (*garantie décennale*) covers any defects which threaten the solidity of the construction or correct functioning of its integral fixtures even if the problem is due to soil subsidence. Plumbers should note that baths are considered integral fixtures. Insurance companies will naturally need to satisfy themselves that foreign applicants have documentary proof of their experience and competence.

The building market is there. Over 50 per cent of homes are owned by their occupants and around 25 per cent of executive classes possess a second home. Foreigners often buy to renovate and it is estimated that around one third of all home owners have some form of modification to their property in mind at any one time.

The competition is also out there. DIY superstores will have their approved list of building contractors and national companies like LaPeyre can install as well as supply their fixtures and fittings for the home. Being able to supply well-presented detailed estimates (*devis*) is vital as people will usually compare at least three estimates, unless strong recommendations are considered more important than a reasonable price. Legally, estimates in duplicate must be prepared for all building maintenance work, breakdown/assistance work or repair work where the amount including VAT (*TVA*) exceeds 150€. Below that amount a written estimate should be supplied if requested. These estimates should be on the business' headed paper and contain at least the following information:

- date and customer details including address where the job would be effected;
- detailed breakdown of materials and unit costs (before and after VAT, and the rate of VAT) and the tax-inclusive total;
- hourly labour rate including rate for fractioned hourly periods, and the tax-inclusive labour total;
- any extras such as transport/delivery charges and whether the estimate is free or to be paid for;
- period for which the estimate remains valid.

Materials and labour may be subject to differing rates of VAT (*TVA*) depending on whether new outside construction work or general improvements are concerned. Set job rates and labour rates should be displayed in premises visited by customers as well as on a rate card if customers are visited at their homes.

Once the business is established, seals of approval from independent organisations printed on estimates will create confidence: *Qualibat* for general building work (www.qualibat.com); *Maître Artisan* (the chamber of trade's seal) and *Qualifelec* (*QE*) for electrical installation companies (www. qualifelec.fr).

Estate agents

Britanny, Normandy, Dordogne, Provence and the Côte d'Azur all have a fair share of estate agencies (*agence immobilières*) which have been started by British people mainly for the international English-speaking market. The Limousin region, as mentioned above, is now becoming increasingly popular with British buyers. It is estimated that 50 per cent of all property purchases by foreigners is in the Mediterranean belt running from Toulon to Menton.

While selling properties as an employee or representative of an *agence immobilière* requires no specific diplomas, owning and running an estate agents requires one of the following:

♦ a diploma in estate agency practice following a course with one of the national federations;
♦ 10 years' salaried experience in estate agencies in France;
♦ four years as manager of an *agence immobilière.*

As with buying a property, locating the business is crucial. Competition is particularly fierce in the Mediterranean area which is full of agencies chasing after fat commissions, which are about double UK rates, on properties which are at least as expensive as their equivalents in South East England.

Export sales agents

With English entrenched as the international business language and the expanding European market, opportunities are there for international sales agents and/or consultants (*agents/conseillers en commerce extérieur*). Export sales agents may find that landing long-term contracts is the main difficulty. As an essential part of initial market research, consult the list of exhibitors at a major trade fair, do your homework and then visit the stands to see what the reactions are to your proposition.

While many French companies that are interested in export or already export will have staff speaking acceptable business English, there is no substitute for someone British who has live contacts, a promise of orders and first-hand knowledge of Northern European markets, including of course the UK. Many companies base their management offices in the Paris area making it easy to keep in touch personally as much of France is now only a few hours from Paris with the TGV high-speed train.

Setting up as an export distributor in France is another matter. It requires a detailed knowledge of export, shipping and documentation practice based on considerable previous experience.

WHAT NAME WILL YOU CHOOSE FOR YOUR BUSINESS?

What name you choose for your business or company and also the brand name (*marque*) for the product or service are also key prior questions. The former will either be the corporate name (*raison sociale*) or sole trader, i.e. your own name (*dénomination sociale*) depending on the type of legal form chosen for the business. Check with an *INPI* office or online at www.inpi.fr that the trading name is not already used in your *département* or any adjacent ones. When you register your business the trading name will become yours. There is, however, nothing to stop it being used as a brand name by another company if you don't use it as a brand name, although 'John Smith', for example, is unlikely to go down well on a national scale.

Choose a short, memorable brand name that encapsulates what the product is or does, having checked on the *INPI* website that the complete name does not already exist. Then register it at an

INPI office. This costs just 215€ (based on 2005 prices) and gives national coverage for the first 10 years. Think in terms of a name that will be readily understood by both Anglophones and Francophones. 'DISCOUNT', 'QUICK', 'SPEEDY', 'EXPRESS', etc. are often used *as part of* business names to indicate the type of product or service offered. For the purely English-speaking market 'FRENCH NEWS' is a complete business name which describes exactly what the newspaper contains. 'BELLIS-SIMMO' is a clever, patented Franco-Italian complete trademark, which most European nationalities will quickly understand and remember making it an ideal name for publicising a small estate agency chain (*agences immobilières*).

WHERE SHOULD YOU SET UP YOUR BUSINESS?

Location is vital if your business relies on passing and local trade. Also, assuming you don't want a long journey to work every day or want to be on the spot in case of out-of-hours emergencies, where you live, or plan to live, will have an important bearing upon the location of your business.

If you live in the country not far from two large towns don't make the mistake of setting up shop in an isolated spot equidistant from each town, in the hope of catching trade from both of them. Far better to opt for a good position in one of the towns or in a well-established shopping centre (*centre commercial*) which may be just out of town. The motorway and main roads network are excellent and most people are within 30 minutes' drive of a *centre commercial*.

Just off a town's high street near major shops is fine for specialist shops such as those selling fishing tackle (a huge market in

France), pet food and equipment (there are almost as many pets as people in France) or ironmongery, ordinary kitchen/tableware and practical novelties (these are very popular as the French are very house-proud). Rents will be cheaper and the premises won't have to be beautifully fitted out.

Tourist businesses traditionally come and go depending upon the seasonal trade and long-term projects should aim for all-year round business. A winter and summer activity such as selling skiing and then hiking equipment in a popular town in the Alps or Pyrenees makes sense. Attractive beach sites are fine when the weather performs, and can produce enough revenue for the whole year, but can be disastrous if there is a bad summer. And many of these sites are subject to annually-awarded municipal permits which are not necessarily renewed for the following year.

Major towns and cities such as Bordeaux, Lyon, Nice, Paris, Strasbourg (with the European Parliament as a tourist attraction) and Toulouse are always full of visiting tourists. Annecy, in Savoy, is one of France's leading tourist towns and Saint Tropez (if you can stand the traffic jams) is a notable exception to the seasonal trade rule as it is always crowded from late spring onwards and throughout the summer months, regardless of the weather.

Look out for trading and industrial estate developments in urban or rural areas if it would be beneficial to your business to be located in one. These estates may be subject (up to the end of 2008 for new businesses) to total or partial tax exemptions on profits, and exemptions from the local business tax (*taxe profes-sionnelle*) – see Chapter 3 – and property tax (*taxe foncière*) – at least for an initial period.

Working from your home may also be a possibility. Regulations and restrictions which apply to working from home and renting, sharing or buying business premises are covered in Chapter 7.

Wherever you are, broadband Internet connection (*Internet haut-débit*) is becoming as important for a variety of businesses as having main utility services laid on. Although France is pre-eminent in broadband expansion check with the local France Télécom office that your computer system can be coupled with the telephone network in the area to give high-speed Internet connection.

WHEN SHOULD YOU START YOUR BUSINESS?

When not to start a business is the real question. Just before and during the *grandes vacances* summer holiday month of August is not a good time regardless of whether your business is going to be local or national. Customers will not be around and if they are, many suppliers – food wholesalers excepted – will be closed and unable to deliver follow-up orders if you get off to a flying start. If other businesses are your main customers, monthly credit terms which coincide with the holiday month of August will automatically extend their credit for another month. The month of May is generally not a good time either as there are usually three or four week-day holidays so you should check the calendar.

Mid-September is a particularly good time, however, when everybody's back to work and thinking of business. Another good time is the start of the New Year after the two-week Christmas break.

UNDERSTANDING EVERYTHING AND BEING UNDERSTOOD

Soul-searching and keeping one's eyes open are sufficient to provide satisfactory answers to the preceding basic questions.

Proceeding to detailed market research, and then entering the worlds of administrative procedures and assistance before launching and running the business will, of course, require a sound command of French.

Even if 95 per cent of future customers are British or Anglophone, or previous employment experience is in the English-language dominated worlds of shipping, motor boat or sailing craft services, official business documents and contracts, and correspondence with public authorities (*l'administration*) must be in immaculate French. Publicity material, such as display posters, which everyone can see, must show the French translation if the verbal message is in English or any other language. Sales letters or publicity leaflet drops to a defined English-speaking market can of course be in English without any translation.

Business letters to a wider market, in French, will require secretarial assistance from a French national – truly bilingual people are extremely rare – and marketing material may require a French specialist to get the message across effectively. This does not mean that your French assistants will have *carte blanche*. It is relatively easy to suggest improvements or spot errors despite the fact that you cannot express yourself as you would wish. Think of artists or draughtsmen drawing up a face or plan for identification with guidance from someone who knows what they want or what they have seen.

Understanding 100 per cent of everything that is said or written is the goal. Everything you say must also be completely understood, even if grammatical errors are always present. Getting the tenses right for verbs is, however, essential. There is not much use in saying you want something to happen if your interlocutor is led to understand that it has already happened.

Form as well as substance is important in French. **Never** use the familiar form of *vous tu* when you are writing to someone in their official capacity, such as the bank manager or the mayor, especially if you're seeking something advantageous, even if you are on first-name terms with them and *'tutoie'* them socially. As a general rule all business letters start with *'Monsieur'* or *'Madame'* and end formally with *'Je vous prie de croire, Monsieur.../Madame...à l'assurance de mes salutations distinguées'*. With this rule, you can't go wrong, although there are other formal letter endings.

The *Alliance Française* (the French equivalent of the British Council) promotes the French language and culture through written and spoken teaching courses and the organisation of inter-cultural functions. The website www.alliancefr.org has details in English and there are about 30 Alliance centres spread throughout France. Ideally, look for qualified teachers in any French-language teaching organisation or university who are ex-business people. If you are in South-East France, Britanny or Normandy the English website www.angloinfo.com has information on language schools in these areas. Visit also www.language-learning.net for details in English – consult French certificate courses – of various business-French courses. The British Embassy (Paris) or the Consulate offices in Amiens, Biarritz, Bordeaux, Boulogne-sur-Mer, Calais, Dinard, Dunkerque, Le Havre, Lille, Lyon, Marseille, Nante and Nice may also suggest websites to consult for information, although they cannot as a government organisation send out addresses for individual schools or give recommendations: www.britishembassy.gov.uk/france. Think of the cost as a business investment. It may also be possible to claim the cost, initially, as a justifiable business expense against tax.

Registered unemployed people with a new business project may qualify for partially or completely subsidised French courses if they already have basic French. State school teachers may offer lessons on a one-to-one basis in their homes which will be cheaper than class lessons given by teachers in private language schools, but the former will not be able to provide invoices for business expense purposes and are unlikely to have a business or technical background.

Practise by yourself, as well. Watching and listening to TV news and weather forecasts provide good comprehension practice and reading the French sub-titles for English-language films on the *Arte* evening channel helps accelerate reading rates. Joining a local sports or recreational club with predominately French members also helps. *Editions Lamy* (www.lamy.fr) publish a pack, with explanatory notes, of 600 ready-made letters and contracts which is a real bible for inexperienced entrepreneurs and foreigners. Lamy also supply registration forms for different legal forms of businesses (see Chapter 3).

USEFUL ADDRESSES

Editions Lamy, 21–23, rue des Ardennes, 75935 Paris Cedex 19. Commercial, company, environmental, insurance, social, taxation and transport law.

Association française de recherches et d'études statistiques commerciales (AFRESCO), 46, rue de Clichy, 75009 Paris.
AFRESCO supplies business information and statistics.

NATIONAL FEDERATIONS

Confédération générale de l'artisanat français, 30, rue des vinaigriers, 75010 Paris.
General federation for self-employed craftsmen/artisans in all types of trades

Confédération générale des petites et moyennes entreprises, 10, terrasse Bellini, 92806 Puteaux. The website, www.cgpme.gov, has information in English.
General federation of small and medium-sized businesses

Confédération de l'artisanat et des petites entreprises du bâtiment, 46, avenue d'Ivry, 75625 Paris cedex 13.
Federation for small construction businesses and building craftsman

Confédération française du commerce de gros et du commerce international, 18, rue des Pyramides, 75001 Paris.
Federation for wholesalers and exporters

Conféderation nationale de l'artisanat, des métiers et des services, 8, impasse Daunay, 75011 Paris.
National federation for craftsman/artisans, service businesses and other trades

Office national interprofessionnel des vins, 232, rue de Rivoli, 75001 Paris.
Professional, national wine-growers' federation

Syndicat des sociétés françaises de conseil et d'assistance au développement international.
SYCADI, 31, avenue Pierre1er de Serbie, 75016 Paris.
Export trade consultant's union

Union professionnelle artisanale, 79, avenue de Villiers, 75017 Paris.
Professional artisans/craftsmens' association

USEFUL WEBSITES
www.afnor.fr
L'association française de normalisation. The French standards association site in English. Links to local offices which can provide full details of regulations and standards for all activities.

www.aprodi.com
Association for industrial development and promotion (association pour la promotion et le développement industriel).

www.coface.fr
The international specialist assuring overseas payment risks. Click on '*nos autres sites*', then scroll down and click on United Kingdom for general information in English about Coface. Click on '*Coface en France*' and then on '*Implantations en France*' for Coface offices in France.

www.fnaim.com
National federation of estate agents and where their member agents are.

www.insee.fr
All the official facts and figures on France's society and economy.

www.ubifrance.fr or www.cfce.fr
International development for businesses (l'agence française pour le développement international des entreprises). Sources for information on export markets, etc.

USEFUL VOCABULARY

brevet	patent
évaluation du fonds de commerce	the value of a business
forme juridique	legal form (of a business)
grandes vacances	summer holidays
Internet haut-débit	broadband connection
taxe professionnelle	local business tax
taxe foncière	property tax

(2)

Getting market research right

REDUCING YOUR RISK THROUGH MARKET RESEARCH

Success in a certain type of business in the UK does not mean it will necessarily be a success on the other side of the English Channel. Or being a successful businessperson in the UK does not mean you will automatically become successful in France. The aim of market research is to test the project and reduce the risk factor as much as possible before launching the company or business. A market research report should be clear and easily readable for you and your advisors and any organisations helping with finance. Use it with the Business Development Plan (see Chapter 4). It should provide both an ideological and practical foundation for your future business.

> *Case study*
>
> *Consider the case history of an extremely wealthy businessperson who originally made his money in the UK, having seized a golden opportunity to supply a large contract that his employer at the time was afraid to take on. As he was nearing retirement age he moved to a tax haven, and more by chance than previous intention, invested heavily in a new soft drink concept (in no way connected with his previous business) by buying the exclusive concession for the neighbouring region and an imposed initial quota of material and stock. The drink proved to have limited appeal and a very short selling season. It was not another golden opportunity. Proper market research before going ahead could have predicted this and indicated that complementary products would be necessary.*

Case study

The case of a restaurant in Les Lecques is, on the other hand, one of those exceptions that proves the rule. Enchanted by this seaside village, between Marseille and Toulon, an Irish-Welsh couple sold up their greengrocery business in England and moved there with no specific business project. After a precarious start making and selling sandwiches, they opened their restaurant, now over 25 years ago, with absolutely no restaurant experience – let alone experience of French cuisine – and hardly able to speak any French. Hard work (they are open all year), persistence and adaptation – the great majority of dishes are Mediterranean and none are typically British – are their ingredients for success.

Case study

A few miles nearer Marseille, the marine carpentry company run by Adrian Byrnes – a New Zealander – with five working associates underlines the importance of previous experience, knowledge of the marketplace, premises and business structure. Charpentiers Réunis Méditerranée (CRM), a limited cooperative company (see *SARL SCOP* in Chapter 3) was created in 1999 in the former ship-building yards in La Ciotat. The associates were all naval carpenters in France seeking independence. By pooling their resources and obtaining outside finance following preparation of a formal business plan showing they had potential customers, they were able, after waiting one year, to open shop in a marine hangar offering nearly 2,000 m^2 floor area. None of the associates would have been able to start up on their own. Their independence is guaranteed by the *SARL SCOP* business structure as no associate or financial partner can have a controlling interest. CRM's niche (which is not without cheaper competition from other Mediterranean countries) is wooden carpentry – as opposed to plastic, composite or metal work – of a high standard. Their restoration work includes listed historic craft.

Case study

Another interesting case is that of Real Land, a UK office development group, which needed to expand their business. They decided to stick to what they knew best – building and letting new office blocks – rather than diversifying into an associated but untried field. France matched their market research criteria: a market with potential, reasonably buoyant, a pleasant country in which to live and not too difficult from an administrative point of view provided that professional consultants and accountants were engaged to ensure everything was set up and administered properly. Some other European countries did not match this criteria. Real Land were able to test the market from the UK, before setting up their limited SARL company in France. Location within France was also well researched. The greater Paris area had too much competition, the Riviera an over supply of office blocks, while the Marseille-Aix-en-Provence-Toulon triangle seemed just right. The company which is run by Nicholas Hill, a Chartered Surveyor, previously with Real Land in the UK, occupies a prime site in modern offices as befits their business. After four years' existence the future looks good. (Nicholas Hill's method for improving his A Level French was very astute. He read Maigret novels in French which he assures keep you guessing right up to the last while providing a good range of vocabulary.)

Organisations such as *Cabinets d'études* (consult *Etudes de marchés* in the *pages jaunes* phone directory or www.pages-jaunes.fr) or Marketing Studies departments of universities provide invaluable and unbiased information, knowing how to present it and how and where to find it. They will, however, not necessarily have previous practical or study experience of the particular product or service. Ideally work with one of them, incorporating your own findings, to produce the final report. See also addresses given at the end of this chapter.

The national business creation agency (*APCE*) claim that the reason for 70 per cent of business failures in the early years is inadequate or no previous market research.

READING YOUR MARKET RESEARCH REPORT

A market research report should produce or confirm the following:

1. The size of your planned market. Is it large enough for your requirements? Can you reach it? Can customers pay for what you are offering?
2. Define or redefine precisely the type(s) of goods or service for different types of customers.
3. Prices that the market will support bearing in mind competition and your projected profit margins. (The French public are particularly good at shopping around for quality products at a good price. They are, however, suspicious if something is too cheap and they are prepared to pay a high, but not exaggerated, price for a de luxe product or service provided they are convinced of the quality.) Below-cost pricing is only authorised for clearance sales and certainly not to launch products. Don't be afraid to use the Internet as a wonderful tool to check out competitive products, their prices and the overall market's growth.
4. Marketing methods, including publicity and advertising and their costs, selling and delivery/distribution. The latter will have a direct bearing on the final choice and locality of business premises.
5. Percentage share of the overall market targeted enabling you to project turnover figures.

Socio-professional and demographic information (as provided by professional Marketing Departments) on potential customers, including buying habits and purchasing power, should be investigated, as should details of market share held by the existing competition (and likely to be obtained by newcomers to the market) and how the former get their business. Overall general factors such as the political and economic climate and likely legislation which could have positive or negative effects should also be taken into account. In 2007 there will be parliamentary and presidential elections.

SOURCING INFORMATION ON YOUR MARKET

If professional assistance is not sought, which is often the case with small business projects on a tight budget, be prepared to spend at least several weeks to do the job properly yourself. A general market survey should first be undertaken, followed by a survey seeking precise information for your product or service, finishing with field research.

The general survey should provide as much information as possible on recent and likely future developments in the general sector which interests you. The situation in a similar sector in the UK that you have just left, or are planning to leave, will not necessarily be the same in France. Similarly, the overall national picture in France may be more *or* less encouraging than your area or *région* if you are only going to operate locally. Read the national and local papers (many of the latter have a weekly economic report looking at prospects and business successes in the area) and of course the trade and specialist magazines. France has a tremendously wide range of magazines and periodicals: probably more than any other country in Europe. And, of course visit Trade and Business Start-up fairs (*Salons professionnels* and *Salons de créations d'entreprises*) for the latest information, ideas and new contacts.

You should then look at your market in detail: its potential; possible customers; the way it's developing and trends (*les tendances*). At this point, officials in trade or professional associations and chambers of commerce should be contacted. They are normally prepared to give free advice, although you may have to pay for reports with market statistics and analyses. Most French administrative set-ups are extremely departmentalised, so don't be put off by initial refusals. Insist politely with your enquiry until you are conducted to the right person. An appointment may of course be necessary. Trade fairs (see above) are very useful in this respect as people manning association and chamber of commerce stands are there to meet people for immediate discussions.

TESTING THE MARKETPLACE

The final step is meeting and testing the marketplace and future customers. On a national scale an opinion-poll company will have to be used if face-to-face discussion with customers is part of the test. If your French is adequate and the future market is local, carry out the poll yourself. It should have multiple choice questions or just a 'yes' or 'no' possibility and avoid asking for a hypothetical buying decision as this can scare people off and encourage 'false' answers. The questionnaire used should be approved or designed by a professional. There's not much point in getting superb answers to the wrong questions! Surveys by phone cover a lot of people in a relatively short period of time. The questions need to be brief and, unless your French is excellent and you're used to telephoning customers, a *télé-marketing* company should be used. Face-to-face polls with more questions than a telephone enquiry will supply in-depth information. On-line 'chat' sessions within appropriate websites also provide rapid answers and information. A combination of all these methods is not a bad idea. Mail shots by post with pre-paid envelopes have notoriously poor return rates, even to well-targeted addresses taken from professional directories or to a purchased potential customer address list that corresponds to your product. (These should not be confused with marketing mailshots as part of your sales promotion activity, once the business is established, which can have good results.)

Is the market information you have obtained sufficiently precise? Does it give detailed figures on the market share for your project enabling a realistic projection of turnover and will you be able to attract customers (and revenue) almost immediately? Even if you have not used or cooperated with a professional person or company to produce the market research report, consider getting it analysed by a specialist business creation company as they will give an unbiased opinion.

USEFUL VOCABULARY

étude de marché	market research
foire	public or trade exhibition or fair
salon	public or trade exhibition or show
télé-marketing	telephone research (or canvassing)
tendances	market trends

USEFUL ADDRESSES AND WEBSITES
General start-up information
APCE, 14, rue Delambre, 75014 Paris.
www.apce.com

National business start-up agency. Information in English, covering procedures, taxation, legal structures, statistics, etc.

Market research

www.syntec-etudes.com

This website provides a list of companies, by geographical area and type of business, carrying out market surveys.

Confédération nationale des juniors entreprises (CNJE), 48, rue Montmartre, 75002 Paris

www.cnje.org

For a list of business students' associations carrying out market surveys. Students are supervised by their lecturers.

Magazines and periodicals

The following publications may provide useful information on market research.

Défis, 204, boulevard Raspail, 75014 Paris
www.entrepreneurs-fr.com

L'Entreprise, 14, boulevard Poissonnière, 75009 Paris
www.lentreprise.com

Challenges, 10–12, place de la Bourse, 75002 Paris
www.challenges.fr

Courrier Cadres, 51, boulevard brune, 75014 Paris
www.apec.fr

Published consumer surveys and economic, financial and statistical information

Credoc, 142, rue du Chevaleret, 75013 Paris

www.credoc.asso.fr

This website provides information on a list of consumer surveys which can be purchased.

Dafsa, 117, quai de Valmy, 75010 Paris

www.dafsa.fr

A company providing information on expensive, but excellent, statistical and economic reports by market/product sectors.

La documentation française, 29, quai Voltaire, 75007 Paris

www.ladocfrançaise.gouv.fr

A website with information provided by the French civil service, which can be borrowed or studied if you are at their office in Paris.

Exhibitions and trade fairs

Fédération des foires et salons de France, 11, rue Friant, 75014 Paris

www.foiresalon.com

This website offers information on dates and venues for forthcoming fairs and exhibitions.

www.salons-online.com

A website providing information on dates and venues for forthcoming trade fairs.

Trade guilds and chambers of commerce

Assemblée des chambres françaises de commerce et d'industrie, 45, avenue d'Iena, 75116 Paris

www.acfci.cci.fr

A good website for addresses of all the chambers of commerce.

Assemblée permanents des chambres de métiers, 12, avenue Marceau, 75008 Paris

www.apcm.com

See this website for addresses of all trade guilds.

3

Forme juridique, social security and taxation

The choice of legal structure (*forme juridique*) most suited to the business project should be made when the business plan (see Chapter 4) has been completed as it is important to have at least a medium-term view of the business' development. Personal and financial responsibilities, day-to-day functioning of the business, social security cover for you, and possibly your spouse (see Employing husbands or wives in Chapter 12) and taxation liability are all factors that can come into play. The conception of the business project should of course not be influenced by the choices of structure available.

Companies outside France seeking to increase or possibly start a business in France should note that:

♦ branch-status businesses in France (*succursales*) which are part of a foreign-registered company do not require to be registered as a legal entity in France; they are, however, subject to French business taxation;

♦ subsidiary-status businesses (*filiales*) of a foreign-registered company must be incorporated under French law and will therefore be subject to company liability and taxation in France. Subsidiaries may apply for state aid (see Chapter 5) when setting up, whereas branches may not;

◆ a market-research office can be set up without any French registration providing no trading is conducted.

Apart from the most well-known legal structures, some of the lesser known ones are described in this chapter, including those particularly suitable for certain types of businesses. Bear in mind that it may be complicated and costly to change to another *forme juridique* if you plan to expand the business later on and bring in associates or partners. Strike up a good relationship with the local tax authorities from the outset by going to see them, rather than trying to obtain advice and information over the phone or by post. As a rule, foreigners who are new to the French business taxation systems are well received.

WHAT *FORMES JURIDIQUES* ARE AVAILABLE?
The table opposite sets out the categories of businesses and professional activities that exist and the choice of structures for them.

Commerçant covers all business activities, notably shops, that buy for selling on at a profit and also the sale of certain services.

Artisan covers the manufacture, modification, transformation and repair of goods or provision of services (*prestations de services*); new *artisan* businesses are limited to employing 10 people, excluding apprentices. Completion of a basic business management course (*stage de gestion*) lasting about a week is obligatory for all future *artisans* unless directly relevant previous experience can be shown. Experienced foreign *artisans* with similar, but not identical experience, gained outside France are advised to still take this course.

Table 3.1 Definitions

The professions	Sole entrepreneur	Two or more entrepreneurs
Licence/diploma required and ruling body	*Entreprise individuelle (EI)* or *Société d'exercice libéral uni-personelle (SELU)*	*Société civile professionnelle (SCP)* *Société d'exercice libéral (SELARL)*
No ruling body, and no licence/diploma required	*Entreprise individuelle (EI)* or *EURL*	*SA, SARL, SAS, SNC*
COMMERCANT **ARTISAN** INDUSTRY	*Entreprise individuelle* or an *EURL*	*Société de personnes:* *SNC, SCOP* *Société en commandité simple* (limited partnerships), *Société en participation* (joint venture company), *Société de capitaux:* *SA, SAS, SARL*

Industrial businesses are those which process or transform raw materials using production machinery and manual labour.

All future entrepreneurs, whether they have already managed a business as a salaried employee in France or set up their own business previously outside France are advised to take some form of business start-up training course. The website www.boutiques-de-gestion.com shows where, when and what type of courses are available through their organisation, throughout France. The national business start-up agency's website www.apce.com is always available and provides step-by-step advice in English throughout all stages of setting up a business. If you are not yet living in France ask the National Centre for Distance Learning (*centre nationale d'enseignement à distance*) to send you details with prices of their business creation (*créer une entreprise*) courses. Their international call centre number is (0033) 5 49 49 94 94 and their website, with an English link is www.cned.fr.

Partners in *commerçant, artisan* and industrial *sociétés de personnes* pay income tax (*IR*) on their proportion of the profits, whereas *sociétés de capitaux* pay corporation tax (*IS*) on the company's profits. Please see the Taxation section in this chapter.

An important choice for someone setting up on their own is whether to opt for *entreprise individuelle*, roughly equivalent to sole trader, or for limited company status as the sole person (*société d'exercice liberal uni-personnelle* or an *EURL*).

Entreprise individuelle (*EI*)

This is the simplest choice and around 60 per cent of new businesses choose it. No minimum capital is required. The business is set up in the name of the entrepreneur as a natural person (*personne physique*) at the appropriate business registration centre (*Centre de formalités des enterprises* (*CFE*)). A trading name (*dénomination commerciale*) may be added. Profits are declared on a personal income tax return form along with any other personal income.

As the activity has unlimited responsibility there is no distinction between business assets and private estate so personal possessions and also those of spouses, depending on the type of marriage contract, or officially registered companions under the *PACS* (see below) system, can be seized by a bailiff (*huissier*) if the business fails.

Marriage or companionship contracts fall into the following categories:

◆ *Communauté universelle.*
   All possessions before and after the marriage are considered as jointly held.
◆ *Séparation des biens.*
   Each spouse retains title to individual possessions acquired before and after the marriage.
◆ *Participation aux acquêts.*
   Allows for the division of future wealth acquired by each spouse in the case of divorce.
◆ *PACS.*
   Male, female or mixed couples retain title to individual possessions acquired before the contract. All possessions acquired subsequently are jointly held in equal parts, unless agreed otherwise in the contract.

If there is no contract accompanying a marriage which was prior to November 1996 all possessions are jointly held (*communauté de meubles et acquêts*), including those pre-marriage. Non-contract marriages after that date are subject to the *communauté réduite aux acquêts*: all post-marriage possessions are jointly held. *Communauté* marriages are therefore not the best solution if an *EI* has financial problems. UK marriages are, however, considered by the French authorities to have been contracted under a *séparation des biens* system. The position regarding Civil Partnerships contracted in the UK or in other European countries with similar civil contracts is unclear at present. Civil partners should check for any possible clarification with a *notaire* (a publicly approved government official) before deciding to become an *EI*.

An important point to note for home owners with their main residence in France is that the law has become more humane, and unsuccessful entrepreneurs are now allowed to keep their home, although they can still lose the furniture in it! A visit to a notary *before* starting the business is necessary so that the private residence is clearly established and protected even if it is ultimately sold, provided the proceeds are used for the purchase of the next home. This registration must be officially published by the *Bureau des Hypothèques* (guarantees office) so that any possible future creditors are aware.

The principal advantage of the *EI* is the complete independence it offers. Outside advice can be solicited but doesn't have to be taken or acted upon. The *EI* is ideal for the one-man band who isn't planning to expand. If the plan is also to just produce a modest annual income, the personal income tax return (the *IR* system) will remain more advantageous than if the business was established as a limited company and subject to corporation tax (*IS*). However, if the business performs very well, the *EI* entrepreneur may find themselves in a higher income tax bracket. Becoming a limited company (*EURL*) and opting to pay tax under the *IS* system could then be considered.

If plans *are* ambitious, continued *EI* status will also not encourage important customers and suppliers to deal with what they will consider to be a small business. Banks and other financial organisations that need to be approached for development finance (see Chapter 6) will not be impressed either.

Sociétés (companies)
This covers all other business structures. Unlike *EIs* they are set up as a legal entity (*personne morale*) – distinct from the founder or founders – with their own name (*dénomination sociale*) and registered head office (*siège social*). The registration procedure for *sociétés* involves notably drafting company articles and recording them with the tax authorities and publishing an official announcement of the new company's existence.

The *société*'s assets are quite separate from the personal estate of its directors if the business fails, except if failure to keep the accounts correctly or deliberate mismanagement (*faute grave de gestion*) has occurred. Dipping into the company's treasury or using assets for personal gain (*abus de biens sociaux*) is a serious offence. Appointed managing directors (*personnes physiques*) act on behalf of the legal entity and submit regular management reports to the associate directors.

Exceptionally, each associate in a cooperative company (*société en nom collective: SNC*) is jointly responsible for company debts. (In practice a *SNC* structure is mainly used by *established* individual entrepreneurs who wish to unite.)

Creating a *société* from the outset is a good choice if decision sharing and working support from others is required. Various structures are available to suit family businesses and partnerships with former colleagues, and also for larger developments involving several working and/or financial partners or where a large initial capital is required. Details of all these are given below. For example, a family *SARL* is ideal for a bed and breakfast business.

Protecting personal estate is also a classic reason for starting a business as a legal entity. Apart from fraud or deliberate mismanagement, personal estate is not protected if it guarantees a bank loan for the business and repayments cannot be met.

Entreprise uni-personelle à responsibilité limitée (EURL)

Along with an *EI*, this is the other *forme juridique* for entrepreneurs that wish to remain independent in deciding how to run their business. An *EURL* can appoint a manager (*gérant*) to run the business on a daily basis while the entrepreneur remains the sole partner (*associé unique*); and in this case some decision taking will be shared. A symbolic minimum initial capital of one euro is required to set up an *EURL*. If a larger initial capital is involved, only 20 per cent has to be deposited immediately with the balance paid over five years.

Unlike an *EI*, the business' assets are separate from the entrepreneur's personal estate. If development of the business necessitates partners and further capital the *EURL* can become a *SARL*. It can also revert to an *EURL*, but not to an *EI* unless the business is officially wound up and then recreated.

The entrepreneur as a *personne physique* automatically pays personal income tax (*IR*) on *BIC* (industrial and commercial) or *BNC* (non-commercial) profits unless they choose, and record their intention, to pay corporation tax profits (*IS*). Book-keeping requirements (see Chapter 10) are more stringent than for an *EI*. While this means more administrative work, it gives a clearer picture of how the business is doing. More *EURLs* survive their first year than *EIs*.

Société anonyme à responsabilité limité (SARL)

This limited company form is the natural step up from an *EURL* as at least two partners are required. Once again, only an initial capital of one euro is required at the outset. In practise organisations providing aid and finance will not be impressed if the strict minimum capital amount is applied. As with *EURLs* if a larger capital is involved, only 20 per cent has to be deposited immediately, with the balance paid over five years. This capital can be in the form of physical possessions or established business contacts brought into the company by one of the partners. If any capital consisting of physical possessions is estimated to exceed 7,500€ or if the total value of this type of capital is thought to exceed 50 per cent of the company's nominal capital a specialised auditor (*commissaire aux apports*) must be instructed for an official evaluation.

All major decisions must be taken at board meetings (*conseils d'administration*) with written-up meetings in special minute books. Any changes to the company's articles must be officially published and notified to the company registrar office (*registre du commerce*). Accounts must be certified annually by an auditor.

The creator of an *EI* or *EURL* which changes to a *SARL* and is the majority shareholder can still effectively control the business.

A company which is formed as a family *SARL* (*de famille*) can opt for *IS* taxation as a *société des capitaux*, like a standard *SARL*, or for IR taxation as a *société des personnes*, just like an *EURL*. The choice should be the right one as it will irrevocably be incorporated in the company's articles which are sent to the tax authorities. It will depend on factors such as the entrepreneur's family situation, anticipated profits and amount of social security contributions. As with a normal *SARL* there must be at least a minimum of two and a maximum of 100 partners whose individual financial responsibility is limited to their capital contribution. The partners in a family SARL must be part of the immediate family – spouse, parents, children, grandparents, brothers, sisters or their spouses.

Qualified professional people working together

The *SCP* (*société civile professionnelle*) is mainly used by the medical professions, although it can be used by other professions which require specific qualifications. The members work in the same premises on a cooperative basis, sharing capital equipment costs and profits depending on individual shareholdings. As with a *SNC*, each member is jointly responsible for company debts.

The *SCM* (*société civile de moyens*) is also mainly used by the medical professions to share capital equipment costs and the same building. Modern, suburban *Espace Santé* (Health Centre) buildings with a common reception area and secretarial service, rented or owned by one of the practitioners, are increasingly replacing old surgeries in town centre buildings. *SCM* members remain individual businesses solely responsible for their own activity.

The *SELARL* (*société d'exercise libéral*) enables members of the regulated professions in all spheres to work together as a *SARL*. Profits are subject to *IS* tax.

Commerçants working together

The *SNC* (previously mentioned) is a structure that can only be used by *commerçants*. It is likely to mainly be of interest to families that get on extremely well together – as everyone concerned is responsible for each other's debts – each with their own trading speciality, and who wish to share premises and equipment. Established businesses which are performing well, with *EI* status, are candidates. At least two partners are required and no minimum capital is required. The company has *unlimited* liability and shares cannot be sold unless partners are unanimously in agreement.

SARL (or SA) SCOP (*société coopérative ouvrière de production*)

This is a *limited* liability cooperative company, suitable for *artisans*, *commerçants*, industrial and service businesses. At least two partners, who are salaried, are necessary for a *SARL SCOP* and at least seven for a *SA SCOP*. Unlike a classic *SARL* no partner can have a majority shareholding and all partners votes are of equal importance regardless of their shareholding. A partner is elected manager and runs the company on a daily basis. *SCOP*s cannot be taken over by any outside financial partner(s) they may have as the salaried partners must together hold at least 51 per cent of the shares.

It is rare to find this structure used for a new business. It is often used by existing employees as a buy-out device in a *SARL* or *SA* to prevent company relocations or dissolutions.

SCS (société en commandité simple)

The principle advantage of this company form for *artisans, commerçants* and industrial entrepreneurs is the provision of capital from a financial partner (the *commanditaire*) for development of an excellent project – which should be backed by a sound business plan – where the entrepreneur has limited funds available or difficulty in raising them. The entrepreneur (the *commandité*) also has a relatively free hand to go about their business while their financial partner limits their involvement to checking over the accounts. A *SCS* has no minimum capital and must have at least two partners: one *commandité* and one *commanditaire*.

While *commanditaires'* risks are limited to their financial contribution, each *commandité* has unlimited joint liability for the company's debts. In this instance, beggars can be choosy, as it is vital that an entrepreneur chooses a financial partner who has confidence in their business ability and will not block development if more finance is required.

Société civile immobilière (SCI)

This is basically a non-trading property holding company set up by several people to jointly buy a property and should *not* be used as a business structure if they want to let out furnished accommodation. Registration, for renting furnished accommodation, is required under the business category of *LMP*: *loueur en meublé professionnel* with *EI, SNC* or family *SARL* legal structures the most appropriate.

Société anonyme (SA)

This is the structure chosen by businesses that plan to expand considerably, possibly via public flotation, becoming roughly equivalent to a Public Limited Company. There must be at least seven shareholders and a minimum starting share capital of 38,000€ of which 50 per cent, if it is cash capital, has to be deposited at the outset with the balance payable over five years. Similar to *SARL*s, a specialised auditor must be used to evaluate physical assets, which must be entirely paid up at the start, if they constitute the capital. Shares can be bought and sold easily depending on the company's financial requirements.

A board of directors of between three and 18 members, including a *président-directeur général* (*pdg*) and perhaps a *directeur général* have to be appointed by a general meeting of the shareholders. Partners and shareholders can only be liable for company debts corresponding to the value of their shares, although directors' personal property can be seized if mismanagement is proved. The *pdg* and *directeur général* are employed as salaried staff regardless of their shareholdings, and, like all salaries, their salaries are deducted before the net profits of the company are declared. Profits are of course subject to *IS* (corporation) tax.

Articles incorporating a *SA* are complex and a corporate lawyer (*juriste* or *avocat*) should be instructed to draw them up. The accounts must be checked by a Chartered Accountant (*expert comptable*).

Société par actions simplifies (SAS)

This limited liability company structure is much more flexible than that of a *SA* and can be used by just one person, as a *SASU* (company with a single shareholder). The *SASU* provides an alternative to an *EURL*. As the minimum starting capital is 38,000€, it is more likely to interest banks and organisations providing finance. 50 per cent of this capital must be deposited at the outset with the balance payable over five years. Transfer from a *SASU* to a *SAS*, i.e. with more than one shareholder, is achieved simply by selling shares. However, it is not possible to open shares to public subscription. A *SAS* would have to become a *SA* to do that.

The articles of incorporation for a *SAS* have inexhaustible possibilities depending on the precise agreement required by the associate shareholders. It is strongly recommended therefore to instruct a corporate lawyer to draw them up in a clear, unequivocal manner. Certain decisions must be unanimously agreed, such as approval of the accounts which must be audited annually; distribution of profits; modification of the capital; company merger, de-merger or dissolution. The company must also have a salaried chairman (*président*) who is usually, but not necessarily, a shareholder.

ABBREVIATIONS AND USEFUL VOCABULARY

CA (chiffres d'affaire)	turnover
commanditaire	sleeping partner
commandité	active or ordinary partner
CFE (centre formalité des entreprises)	business registration procedures office
GEIE (groupement européen d'intérêt économique)	European affiliated group of companies

GIE (groupement intérêt économique)	affiliated group of companies
IR (impôt sur le revenu des personnes physiques)	personal income tax
IS (impôt sur les sociétés)	corporation tax
président	chairman
RCS (registre des commerces et des sociétés)	business and companies register
société de fait	unregistered company
RJ (redressement judiciaire)	receivership
SCA (société en commandité par actions)	limited partnership company with at least 38,000€ initial capital
SELCA (société d'exercice libérale en commandité par actions)	limited partnership company for the regulated professions with at least 38,000€ initial capital
SELU (société d'exercice libérale uni-personnelle)	one-man limited company for the regulated professions
SEM (société d'économie mixte)	an *SA* with majority public and minority private capital set up to create and manage a local/regional service or establishment of general interest to the community

SOCIAL SECURITY AND UNEMPLOYMENT BENEFIT

Would-be creators or partners in new businesses were in the past often discouraged by the lack of unemployment benefit cover available for them if they were unsuccessful. Private assurance is now available at reasonable rates to provide unemployment benefit.

Classification as salaried or non-salaried depends on the business structure chosen and in companies it also depends on the shareholding and/or management position held. Whether salaried or not, all entrepreneurs in France (unlike the UK) must make payments into either a basic scheme or basic and complementary scheme to provide minimum social security cover. The *président directeur général* and *directeur général* of *SA*s, minority or egalitarian shareholders in a *SARL*, and manager (with an employment contract) in a *SNC* are salaried. An *EI* entrepreneur, sole partner in an *EURL*, majority shareholder in a *SARL*, and director of a *SNC* are not salaried.

Non-salaried entrepreneurs can now ask for social security payments for their initial year's activity, to be deferred for 12 months and then paid in equal instalments over the following five years. The set minimum rates, which are not the same for *commerçants*, *artisans*, and other service and professional activities, are applied during this first year.

Both salaried and non-salaried classifications are reimbursed at the same rate by the health service – which everyone must contribute to – for visits to doctors and dentists. Top-up medical cover with a *mutuelle* (see also Chapter 11) is recommended, although premiums for non-salaried people are higher than those for salaried people.

Retirement pension is composed of the basic pension, a complementary pension and a supplementary pension. Everyone must pay into the basic pension scheme. This pension has an upper limit of around 1,200€ a month which will only be attained by those who have paid contributions into the French system for 160 quarterly periods and have sufficiently high previous average annual earnings. UK male entrepreneurs will still have to wait until they are 65 to ensure they get the best possible basic pension from the British and French systems. A complementary pension scheme is obligatory for all salaried people and contributions are made to the *ARRCO* organisation, and executives (*cadres*), which will be the case with salaried company directors, shareholders – other than majority ones – and managers, also pay into the special *AGIRC* pension scheme. *Artisans* must contribute to the *CANVACA* organisation and other non-salaried professional groups contribute to the *CNAVPL* organisation. A complementary pension scheme is not obligatory for *commerçants*. Supplementary pension schemes are optional, through savings plans or insurance policies.

Unemployment benefit *may* be accorded by the *ASSEDIC* organisation if businesses fail and only to the following:

- a manager, without any shares, with an employment contract in an *EURL*;
- a minority shareholding manager or a partner in a *SARL*, with an employment contract;
- a salaried *pdg* or *directeur général* of a *SA*, with an employment contract.

The contract should be approved by the *ASSEDIC before* making unemployment benefit contributions for the people concerned. In the case of 'refusal' by the *ASSEDIC*, and for all other entrepreneurs, private unemployment benefit assurance should be considered with either the *GCS* or *APPI* organisations. You should apply for insurance from the start – don't wait until it may be refused if the accounts show that the business is struggling. An entrepreneur who left salaried employment to start a business or who was previously registered as unemployed is also entitled to unemployment benefit from the *ASSEDIC* if their business fails within three years.

ABBREVIATIONS AND USEFUL ADDRESSES

APPI (association pour la protection des patrons indépendants), 25, boulevard de Courcelles, 75008 Paris.

GSC (garantie sociale des chefs d'entreprise), 42, avenue de la grande Armée, 75017 Paris.
www.gsc.asso.fr

AGIRC (associations générales des institutions de retraites de cadres)
Special additional complementary pension funds organisation for executive staff only.

ARRCO (associations des régimes de retraite complémentaire)

Complementary pension funds organisation for executive and non-executive staff.
www.agirc.fr – joint website for AGIRC and ARRCO – the website is in French only. AGIRC ARRCO, 16–18, rue Jules César, 75592 Paris cedex 12. Tel: 01 71 72 12 00.

CANAM (caisse nationale d'assurance maladie et maternité des professions indépendants)
National fund for sickness and maternity benefit payments for the self-employed who provide a service, as opposed to manufacturing, or trading, goods.
Visit www.canam.fr for examples of social security contributions.

CANCAVA (caisse autonome nationale de compensation de l'assurance vieillesse des artisans):
www.cancava.fr
National pension fund for self-employed artisans/craftsman.

CNAVPL (caisse nationale d'assurance vieillesse des professions libérales):
www.cnavpl.fr
National pension fund for self-employed who provide a service, as opposed to manufacturing, or trading, goods.

ORGANIC (organisation autonome nationale d'assurance vieillesse de l'industrie et du commerce):
www.organic.fr
National life insurance, retirement and pension fund for non-salaried workers in industry and commerce.

In January 2006 the RSI organisation was created, merging the CANAM, CANCAVA and ORGANIC organisations. *Artisans* and *commerçants* now pay their social security contributions for pensions, disability and life cover (*vieillesse, invalidité, décès*) into the RSI which administers funds and dispenses benefits.

Social security registration offices for writers, artists and composers:

AGESSA (association pour la gestion de la sécurité sociale des auteurs) 21 bis, rue de Bruxelles, 75009 Paris. www.agessa.org

Maison des artistes, 90, avenue de Flandre, 75019 Paris. www.maisondesartistes.org

TAXATION

The way profits and the entrepreneur's income are taxed, as well as taxation rates and brackets, vary depending on the business structure and also on the annual turnover.

Impôt sur le revenu (IR) or sur les sociétés (IS)

There are two main situations: *EI*s, where profits are inextricably part of the entrepreneur's personal income and thus subject to *IR* taxation, and companies, where the directors' remuneration and dividends are also subject to *IR* taxation and taxed separately from company profits, subject to corporation (*IS*) taxation.

EI profits are industrial and commercial profits (*BIC*), or non-commercial profits (*BNC*) for all other service and professional categories. Company profits – after the deduction of directors' income – are subject to *IS* taxation at a basic rate of 34.33 per cent. A reduced rate of 15.45 per cent applies on profits up to the first 38,000€ provided that the business' last turnover figures were below 7,630,000€ *HT* (exclusive of VAT) and that all the company capital was paid up initially with at least 75 per cent provided by individual people (*personnes physiques*).

Although the legal structure usually determines how profits and entrepreneurs' income will be taxed, in the case of an *EURL* or family *SARL* either *IS* or *IR* taxation is an option. The taxation

choice must be written into the company's articles of incorporation and communicated to the taxation authorities *before* the
business starts, which is another reason why a business plan
should be completed at this stage. It will be difficult to forecast
profits otherwise. If a new business is likely to enjoy tax exemptions (see *Zones franches urbaines* in Chapter 7) it will be more
interesting to choose *IS* as the exemption applies to the entire
profits and directors' earnings.

With *EI*s, actual business expenses are deducted when making tax
returns which are classed as *régime réel simplifié* or *régime réel
normal*, according to the type of business and annual turnover. *EI*s
classed as a *micro-entreprise* have set business expenses tax
allowances. The tax rate for all *EI*s corresponds to a sliding *IR*
scale which varies depending on whether the entrepreneur has
income from other sources and their family situation. A major
reform simplifying the *IR* taxation system was recently voted and
will be effective from 2007, applying to income in 2006. *IR* tax
will be less onerous and more in line with neighbouring European
countries. The highest *IR* tax band will be annual taxable income
over 65,500€, subject to 40 per cent tax, whereas annual taxable
income for 2005 over 48,748€ attracted 48 per cent tax. Annual
taxable income between 24,433 and 65,500€ will be taxed at 30 per
cent, annual taxable income between 11,001 and 24,332€ at 14 per
cent, and annual taxable income between 5,515 to 11,000€ at
5.5 per cent. Up to 5,514€ taxable income there will be no taxation.

Régime réel simplifié

This applies to all *EI*s and companies with annual sales turnover
between 76,300 and 763,000€ *HT* or between 27,000 and
230,000€ *HT* annual turnover if they provide a service.

Régime réel normal

This applies to all *EI*s and companies with annual sales turnover over 763,000€ *HT* or over 230,000€ *HT* if they provide a service. Accounting obligations are more onerous than with the *régime réel simplifié*.

Micro-entreprise

This is a most advantageous form of taxation *régime* which applies to turnover and not profits, and many small businesses will find it suits them. Accounting obligations are limited to recording receipts and expenses in a *Recettes Dépenses* daybook and simply completing an *IR* tax return form annually. To qualify, businesses must have an annual sales turnover (and furnished accommodation rental income is included in this category) of less than 76,300€ *HT* or a turnover of less than 27,000€ *HT* if they provide a service. VAT cannot be included on invoices and the following must be stated on invoices: '*TVA non applicable, art. 293B du CGI*'. The fixed business expenses tax allowances which apply, regardless of actual expenses incurred, are 72 per cent off the higher (sales turnover) category, 52 per cent for service businesses subject to *BIC* taxation, and 37 per cent for *BNC* service businesses. *IR* taxation is applied to the resulting net figures.

Déclaration contrôlée or régime du bénéfice réel

This *régime* applies to *BNC* service businesses which invoice VAT (*TVA*) and have an annual turnover above the *micro-entreprise* limit of 27,000€ *HT*. Profits are taxed directly with no set business expense allowances.

The table opposite will help non-salaried entrepreneurs decide which taxation system to choose.

Table 3.2 Turnover figures and choice of taxation system

	Turnover threshold	How to calculate profits	VAT	Accounting obligations	Deficits taken into account on household income for tax purposes	20 % allowance on taxable profits if member of CGA/AGA accounting organisation	Cost of CGA/AGA offset against tax
Micro Entreprise (*BIC*)	Under 27,000€ services Under 76,300€ others (excl. VAT)	Turnover, less 52% Turnover, less 72%	No No	Simplified. No balance sheet or annual accounts necessary	No	No	No
Micro Entreprise (*BNC*)	Receipts under 27,000€ (excl. VAT)	Receipts, less 37%	No	Simplified tax returns	No	No	No
Régime réel (*BIC*)	Over 27,000€ services Over 76,300€ others	Costs deducted from sales	Paid on sales. VAT paid on costs is paid back.	Complex: balance sheet, annual accounts, detailed tax return.	Yes	Yes	Yes
Déclaration contrôlée (*BNC*)	Receipts over 27,000€ (excl. VAT)	Costs deducted from receipts	Paid on sales. VAT paid on costs is paid back.	Complex: balance sheet, annual accounts, detailed tax return.	Yes	Yes	Yes

Imposition forfaitaire annuelle (*IFA*)

All *IS* taxation businesses must pay this annual turnover tax before the 15th March each year unless their turnover is below 76,000€ inclusive of VAT. There is a sliding tax bracket scale calculated on turnover, regardless of whether the business has made a profit or loss, with a maximum *IFA* bracket for turnover of at least 76,000€. The current (2006) taxes for businesses with turnover between 76,000 and 149,000€ and between 150,000 and 299,000€ are 750€ and 1,125€ respectively. Companies in development areas which are exempt temporarily from *IS* tax and companies with at least half of their capital as cash do not pay *IFA*.

VAT (*TVA*)

TVA (*taxe sur la valeur ajoutée*) at the rate of 19.6 per cent applies to the great majority of goods and services, with the notable exception of food, books, transport, officially-rated tourist hotels, country gîtes, camp sites and home improvement work (to properties over two years old), where the rate is 5.5 per cent. There is a strong movement for a reduction to 5.5 per cent for restaurant meals. Although at the end of 2005 France was once again unsuccessful in obtaining European Union agreement to this. Newspapers and those medicines which are reimbursed by the health service are subject to a reduced rate of 2.1 per cent. All export transactions are zero rated.

♦ New businesses pay *TVA* as they go – monthly during the first 12 months.

♦ Businesses subject to *régime réel simplifié* taxation subsequently pay *TVA* in three quarterly advance instalments (April, July, October) which are each 25 per cent of the previous 12 months' TVA, with a final quarterly (December) instalment of 20 per cent.

They can, however, ask to transfer to the *régime réel normal*, just for *TVA* monthly payments, provided this is officially notified within 3 months of starting the business to the appropriate CFE or tax authorities.

◆ Businesses subject to *régime réel normal* taxation continue to pay TVA monthly.

Taxe professionnelle

This local business tax is calculated on the value of fixed assets used for or by the business such as property and equipment and also on a small per centage of business revenue. The taxation rates can vary considerably between neighbouring communities. All non-salaried individual entrepreneurs and all companies are liable except certain types of artisans, farmers, writers and artists, and private schools. Designated development areas offer temporary or permanent exemption. Double-check with tax authorities that any amount due is correct. Don't hesitate to put in a justifiable claim as considerable rebates are successfully obtained every year.

IS taxation and associations (Loi 1901)

Charitable organisations or leisure activities organisations must be registered as an *association* under this old law to account for the receipt and expenditure of annual subscriptions and contributions. However, an *association* can also be set up to test a business idea before deciding whether or not to proceed to a business structure. It will be subject to *IS* taxation on any profits. Payments received from the sale of goods and services must not exceed 38,000€ and any after-tax profits must be ploughed back into the *association*.

WHY NOT REGISTER AS A UK COMPANY?

Registering as a UK limited company is a great deal simpler than registering a company in France. International consultants (look under *conseils en organisation, gestion* ... in the *Page Jaune* directory) such as Ernst and Young, have bilingual experts who can advise you if your business is appropriate. Basically, the business must be able to show a regular amount of business coming from the UK. From a commercial point of view, if the main market is French, customers may be discouraged from dealing with a 'Ltd.' company. Plus any potential future French employees will be unhappy if they are not offered the advantages that contribution to the French social security system provides.

Case study

An interesting case is that of British Connexion Limited with a subsidiary company registered in France. Accounts are done in the UK and France for the respective companies. This family company publishes the monthly English-language newspaper *The Connexion* which is bought in France by expatriates, and in England and other Anglophone countries by lovers of France and/or people with a second home in France or plans to move there. *The Connexion* was created four years ago as a business working from home in France and provides up-to-date practical information and news from France. The idea came from practice when the founders realised questions they had about life in France were shared by others living there too. Contributing journalists around France work remotely with the Editor.

4

What sort of business plan?

Why you should have a business plan might well be the first question to ask.

Here are two good reasons. Both reasons assume that the idea is to start a business with the firm intention to come through the critical early years and continue afterwards.

- If banks and/or financial partners are required to help finance the project from the outset, they will want to know and see in a clearly presented form exactly what is involved, with projected results, so that they can give the proposal their best consideration.
- Even if no outside finance is involved, a carefully prepared business plan will plot out the objectives and which ones to keep the right side of, on the necessary route to success and also convince key suppliers, with whom you're seeking generous credit terms, of the business' viability.

The business plan should, of course, be in French if it is going to be presented to organisations and suppliers, and professional help from a specialist company (consult *conseils et études* in the *Page Jaune*) will almost certainly be necessary. They will have experience of clear, positive and attractive presentation, and of getting the content just right and expressed in concise French. A foreigner who has had no experience at all of running his/her own business, despite considerable managerial experience, is unlikely to be able to present a project as convincingly as a specialist company's presentation. That said, the initial draft should come from the entrepreneur who is the only person, at least to begin with, to know what the project is all about. Take time over this and only present it to your professional helpers to check-over the project description and lay-out when completely satisfied with the draft. The financial details will almost certainly have to be drawn up by an accountant.

The plan should be a 'selling' tool containing the following elements:

♦ summary;
♦ presentation of the entrepreneur (and his associates);
♦ general presentation of the product or service;
♦ financial details.

You should also include appendix documents which may be available such as the company articles, agreed sources of finance, official references from independent professionals, firm commitments from future customers, etc.

SUMMARY

Like a good novel (except it's a real plan) the summary (*résumé*) should arouse interest immediately and in a sense it is the most important document. It is recommended that the summary is no longer than two pages.

PRESENTATION OF THE ENTREPRENEUR

The presentation *(présentation du ou des porteurs de projet)* is an adaptation of a classic CV. As everything is known about the (future) business concerned by the 'candidate' entrepreneur(s), only personal skills and previous employment experience which are directly relevant to the nature of the business and its objectives should be shown. Personal motivation – don't overdo it – should also be included in this document as well as details of any professional studies and courses which support the presentation. The latter might include completion in France of a basic business management course (see page 35 in Chapter 3) and/or certificates showing practical knowledge of the products or services the business will market.

PRESENTATION OF THE PRODUCT

The product presentation *(présentation d'informations générales sur le projet)* can be split into three parts:

1. A description of the revenue-producing product/service, and any patent taken out, with material and any staff required.
2. A brief survey of the market, its trends and competition and reserve or contingent plans. If you have a market research report (see Chapter 2) indicate that this is an annexe document.
3. An outline of marketing strategy, not forgetting to cover sector and market-share objective, pricing policy, distribution channels and publicity methods.

Use the following checklist to prepare the information which is usually expected:

- Business name, legal form, address and telephone number.
- Business capital with shareholding details.
- Personal details of the entrepreneur:
  - Full name, maiden name, date of birth.
  - Marital status, number of children at home, marriage contract, especially if married in France, and level of responsibility for spouse's debts.
  - Relevant employment experience.
  - Appropriate skills and/or independent aptitude report from an official organisation.
  - Current employer or situation.
  - Current income (income tax return may be asked for).
  - Details, with amounts, of outstanding loans.
  - Relevant training and certificates.
- Spouse's details:
  - Employment.
  - Income.
  - Will he/she be working in the business?
- The project:
  - Planned start date.
  - Product or service details.
  - The market.
  - Competition.
  - Staff structure (if applicable).
  - Premises (location, size, leased or purchased).
  - Office equipment, machinery (provide estimates if finance required).
  - Payment terms for customers and credit terms with suppliers. (size of major suppliers and possible major customers may be requested).

FINANCIAL DETAILS

The financial nuts and bolts of the business plan (*dossier financier*) should have four component surveys:

- setting-up costs and funds available
- forecast results for first three years
- three-year financial plan, and
- first 12 months' cash-flow breakdown.

Taken together these should show, ideally, sufficient income and resources for healthy business development over the first three years. They should at the same time be realistic and precise as possible, allowing for teething problems or hiccups such as having to modify the product or re-think publicity if the initial campaign doesn't work Businesses don't usually run exactly to plan. As a foreigner and/or a newcomer to starting and running a business you will need to make special efforts to master French business terms and/or understand business finance so that you know and understand, and can be seen by financial organisations and business people to know and understand, what you are talking about. (Bear in mind also that three years' certified accounts will be expected by potential buyers if the business is put up for sale in the future.)

Here are simplified examples of lay-out for these surveys and items to be included in each:

Setting-up costs/funds (Bilan de depart)

If the *besoins* total is more than the *ressources* total another loan at sensible interest rates will be necessary to show a positive balance.

Costs/*Besoins*

Fixed assets/*immobilisation* (cost of premises, fittings, machinery, office equipment, company vehicles, etc.)

Cash flow situation (value of warehouse stock for products, plus amounts due/*créances* from customers, minus amounts due /*crédits* to suppliers).

Cash, in trading account/ *solde en banque*

Total

Funds/*Ressources*

Deposited company capital/ *capital social* and current account registration costs, holdings of directors in limited companies, or amount provided by entrepreneur/ sole trader

Grants and subsidies (*subventions*) awarded

Loan details and repayment periods/*emprunts*, overdraft facility

Total

Forecast for first three years (*Comptes de resultat sur trois ans*)

In the same way that three-year results are expected from any would-be future buyers, the first three years forecast is the document most closely examined by financial organisations. While you may be able to produce a skeleton forecast based on a market research report, ask an accountant to check that all appropriate items are included and that the figures are realistic if there are any guesstimates. (This type of service may be available free through associations for *conseil à la création des entreprises*.)

	Year 1	Year 2	Year 3

Turnover/*chiffre d'affaires*
excluding *TVA* (*HT*)

Goods, services, rental income
(*marchandises, produits, productions
de biens, prestations de services*, etc.)

Total _____

Purchases: raw materials, stock/
*achats: matières premières,
marchandises*

Outgoings/*charges*

   Subcontracting (*sous-traitance*)

   Leasing agreement (*crédit-bail*)

   Rent (*loyer*)

   Electricity, water, gas

   Maintenance costs

   Accountant (*honoraires comptable*)

   Publicity budget

   Travel expenses (*déplacement*)

   Phone, post, Internet, etc.

Gross salaries (*salaires bruts*)
Employer's social security payments
(*charges sociales patronales*)
Director's remuneration
(if applicable)

	Year 1	Year 2	Year 3

Local business tax (*taxe professionnelle*), if applicable

Loan interest (*intérets sur emprunts*)

Bank charges (*agios*)

Depreciation (*amortissements*)

Total _____

Turnover – Purchases and Outgoings   _____
= pre-tax profits/*bénéfice avant impôts*

Profits tax (*IS* or *BIC/BNC*)   _____

Net profit (*bénéfice net d'exploitation*)   _____

If you work from home the general rule is to allow for 33 per cent of gas, heating, water, electricity, rent (if applicable) and maintenance costs for your property as business outgoings. A more precise percentage corresponding to the overall floor area your office or workshop covers in relation to the property is necessary if this is obviously more than a third.

Three-year financial plan (Plan de financement sur trois ans)

This sets out the resources available throughout this period against the business' financial needs (*besoins*). The year's balance is the resources total minus the financial needs total. The cumulative balance will show if any previous year's deficit is made up in the following year. Cash flow requirements (*besoin en fonds de roulement (BFE)*) usually vary from year to year and the forecast difference for this item in the financial plan may be a financial need (if the requirement increases) or a resource (if the needs are less) in the following year. In the following simplified example of a three-year financial plan the cash-flow requirement (*besoins*) increases in Year 2 by 1,000€ (to 5,000€) and in Year 3 by a further 800€ (to 5,800€).

There are no loans in this example but there is a small grant entitlement, after three years, of 1,000€ towards the cost of replacing essential machinery and vehicles. This is a healthy example of a financial plan showing adequate resources to cover the business' development over the crucial first three years with sufficient funds for re-investment in capital goods.

	Year 1	Year 2	Year 3
Financial needs/*besoins*			
Registration costs	3,000€	–	–
Investments (machinery, vehicles, etc.)	5,000€	–	10,000€
Cash-flow requirements	4,000€	1,000€	800€
Total	12,000€	1,000	10,800€
Resources/*ressources*			
Grants, subsidies (*subventions*)	–	–	1,000€
Company capital and bank account holdings	11,000€	–	–
Year's operating profit allowing for depreciation amounts (*marge brute d'autofinancement: MBA*)	2,000€	8,000€	8,000€
Total	13,000€	8,000	9,000€
Year's balance/*solde de l'année*	1,000€	7,000€	–1,800€
Cumulative balance/*solde cumulé*	1,000€	8,000€	6,200€

Cash-flow plan (Plan de tresorerie)

The layout model below shows on a month-by-month basis how receipts and outgoings can be set out and will be particularly useful for businesses that have seasonal peaks of income or who have customers that enjoy extended credit terms or are slow payers. Negative balance periods will therefore be anticipated and suitable temporary overdraft facilities can be negotiated if necessary, and in advance, with bankers so that fixed-period payments common to all businesses, such as monthly salaries and quarterly *TVA* and social security contribution payments can be met.

The annual plan totals all income and outgoings and will also show the break-even point (*seuil de rentabilité/point mort*) for the new business: the point at which gross profit covers fixed costs. Realistic break-even point figures can attract additional finance if this is required for long-term development.

Jan Feb Mar Apr May Jun Jul Aug Sep Oct Nov Dec

Balance/*solde*
at beginning of month

Receipts/*encaissements*
– from turnover
– from company capital,
  bank a/c holdings
– from any loans
  Total A

Operating payments
/*décaissements*

Jan Feb Mar Apr May Jun Jul Aug Sep Oct Nov Dec

- purchases (raw
  materials, stock, etc.)
- sub-contracting
- leasing agreement
- rent
- electricity, water, gas
- maintenance costs
- gross salaries
- social security payments
- phone, post, Internet
- *TVA* payments
- local business tax
  (if applicable)
- profits tax

Other costs
- loan interest
- depreciation

Total B _____

Monthly balance _____
(A – B)

Cumulative balance _____

USEFUL VOCABULARY AND DEFINITIONS

bilan	general term for statement of accounts
compétence	professional skill
diplôme	certificate
équipement industriel	industrial plant
frais	expenses
plan de développement	business plan
produit	apart from the classic meaning of an article/good(s)/product, accountancy jargon covering visible and invisible earnings
régime matrimonial	(pre) marriage settlement contract
véhicule de fonction	company vehicle, not for weekend or private use

5

Advice, information, aid, grants and loans

A wide range of independent federations and public bodies giving free or paid-for advice, state-aid organisations, and no-interest loans (*prêts d'honneur*) exist throughout France, at national (sometimes European), regional and *département* levels. State aid for the unemployed who want to start a business, including low-interest loans, is also available. Private sources for funds, classic bank loans and venture capital are discussed in Chapter 6, and financial advantages and tax relief which are linked to location and certain development areas are covered more fully in Chapter 7.

Whatever the requirement, it is essential that information forms are filled in correctly and all requested documents supplied, and with the exact number of copies required. Otherwise all paperwork may be returned or the application filed pending receipt of the missing items. This is particularly important for state aid as processing applications can take months rather than weeks. Note that an ✗ is the affirmative symbol when replying to questions and not a ✔

While you will usually get a sympathetic, helpful and open-minded hearing from bodies managing public funds for loans and grants, correctly completed application forms will not of course guarantee a favourable decision. These funds are subject to strict budgets. Convincing, well-argued applications with realistic figures always help. It may not be possible however to accumulate grants and loans even if they are funded from different sources.

ADVICE AVAILABLE

Agences de développement et comités d'expansion économiques

These economic development agencies which come under the banner of the national committee for regional economies are non-profit making *associations* throughout France which can help and advise with preparation of a project and a business plan. They also organise seminars on aspects of the regional economy. See the website www.cner-france.com or chambers of commerce to locate the local association.

The *EGEE* association

This was developed as a means of bringing together business management experience from different age groups using working and retired people. It specialises in small businesses and industries (*PME* and *PMI*) providing guidance and assistance for administrative procedures, choice of legal form of the business, obtaining finance and preparing business development plans. Write to Egée, 15 avenue de Ségur, 75007 Paris or consult www.egee.asso.fr.

Boutiques de gestion

These are not to be confused with *associations/centre de gestion agrées* which are described in Chapter 7.

The national federation for these *boutiques* has members in nearly all *départements* in France offering advice and training on all aspects of business creation, contact with other future entrepreneurs and continued help, if desired, up to two years after starting up. Initial consultation is free and the cost of further advice depends on each applicant's financial situation. Write to the Comité de liaison des Boutiques de gestion, 14, rue Delambre, 75014 Paris or consult www.boutiques-de-gestion.com.

Chéquiers-conseil

Counselling coupon books are available free to registered unemployed people and certain other groups who meet the necessary requirements to be considered for financial assistance under the *ACCRE* (see page 76) system.

The *chéquier* contains six coupons, each worth around 46€ entitling the holder to an hour's consultation with approved specialists such as notaries and accountants who will advise on specific aspects of the project before trading begins or in the early life of the business. (Coupons can be asked for up to three years after the start of a business.) The coupon book holder just has to pay the difference, approximately 16€, of the set hourly consultation rate of about 62€. Each coupon book is date stamped when obtained from the *départemental* employment office (*Direction départementale de travail*) and is valid for 12 months. Up to two coupon books, i.e. 12 hours' consultancy, is the entitlement, before starting a business, and up to three books, minus any books used before the business' start date, *provided* that the entrepreneur has been awarded *ACCRE* assistance.

INFORMATION AVAILABLE

The Business Start-up Agency (*Agence pour la création d'entreprises: APCE*)

This agency will not give a personal counselling service, but its website (www.apce.com), with introductory sections in English, is full of facts and figures about France and information on formal business procedures. It also directs you, by geographical area, to the organisation or chamber of commerce you should contact for further information depending on whether you have a commercial or industrial project, *artisanal* or agricultural project and depending upon your employment situation. The *APCE* estimate that new businesses that use training and consultation organisations have a 30 per cent better chance of success than those businesses which go it entirely alone.

TCE

Le Train de la Création d'Entreprises (*TCE*), now in its fourth year, was set up under the patronage of the government financial and small businesses Ministries in association with *Le Figaro* newspaper, *L'Entreprise* business magazine and the *Salon des Micro Entreprises* (small businesses exhibition). The train tours major cities throughout France with an all-day stop in the main station, and has accountants and lawyers on board giving free consultations, advice and information; business assurance and computer software companies, and representatives from Chambers of Commerce.

Talks are also given on themes such as business plans and choice of legal form for new businesses. All information is in French only. Visit www.traincreationentreprises.com for full information including the train's itinerary.

Other useful government websites:

www.pme.gouv.fr
For small- to medium-sized businesses, *commerçants*, *artisans* and the professions.

www.minefi.gouv.fr
Ministry of Economy, Finance and Industry

www.entreprises.minefi.gouv.fr
Information from the above ministry for enterprises.

How to become a franchisee

The *FFF* (*la féderation française de la franchise*) (website: www.franchise-fff.com) has useful introductory information in English. You should consider the advantages of buying a well-tried and profitable business formula and association with a successful trade mark – while remaining an independent business structure – and also the minimal cost of participation in national advertising campaigns to consolidate brand image and launch new products. France is, perhaps surprisingly, the biggest franchise market in Europe. The market is worth about 45€ billion, which is almost twice Germany's market and nearly three times Britain's market. Although franchisees have a lower risk element than completely independent entrepreneurs the returns are generally lower. If a move to France is dependent upon buying a franchise be prepared to move to where the best opportunity is, although this may not be where you have always enjoyed spending your holidays. Beware also of being exploited by a franchiser in a new area to test the market.

Franchises usually demand heavy commitment in terms of time and initial investment, plus you may need to live close by to supervise the business, even if you're not working in it on a daily basis. Teething troubles, which can otherwise be costly with an un-tried business, are mostly avoided and displaying a franchise on a business card assures a good *entrée* to banks.

Franchisees can generally get on with their business knowing that any technical or operational problems that do crop up can be quickly solved from the franchising company's previous experience. That said, quiz other franchisees in the same business to see how they're doing: did the training meet their expectations? Does the franchiser provide the support expected, when required? Does the franchisee have any regrets?

The *FFF* (*fédération française de la franchise*) 60, rue de la Boétie, 75008 Paris, website: www.franchise-fff.com, has useful introductory information in English and it organises a two-hour initial information session which costs around 40€. There is also a separate day-long seminar, costing around 190€, for more detailed information.

AID AVAILABLE
ACCRE (l'aide aux chômeurs créateurs d'entreprises)
This is a state aid subject to case-by-case approval, or refusal, for the registered unemployed and other categories of people who can show limited means or special circumstances. Twelve months exemption from social security contributions up to a certain income level (with the exception of contributions to the complementary pension scheme) and continued payment of unemployment benefit, generally for six months and in the case of

state widows' benefit for 12 months, are the initial financial advantages for new businesses. Application forms are available from the *Direction départementale de travail* (see *chéquiers-conseil* above) and must be correctly completed and returned before registering any business. Application for *ACCRE* cannot be made once trading has begun. Send the application by recorded delivery or ask for a receipt if it is delivered by hand. Successful *ACCRE* candidates may also qualify for an *EDEN* loan with professional advice (see page 85).

ANVAR

As well as possible tax relief, new industrial and commercial businesses proposing innovative products or systems may qualify for a grant or interest-free loan. The national agency for research and development (*ANVAR*) funds up to 70 per cent of research and development costs and loans can be written off if the project fails. There are 25 regional offices. Write to ANVAR, 43, rue de Caumartin, 75436 Paris cedex 09 or visit website www.anvar.fr.

Aid from regional funds (*fonds regionauxa d'aide au transfert de technologie*) also exists for small new industries (*PMIs*) for research and technical training.

CAPE (contrat d'appui au projet d'entreprise)

Introduced by the economic initiative law in 2003 this provides a generous test period of up to three consecutive years. The period can extend over one, two or three separately agreed 12 month periods for individuals wishing to test out their business idea.

The element of initial risk is greatly reduced as the future entre-preneur is taken in hand by a company or association (*couveuse*) providing them with a supervised training programme geared to their project. The course is full-time and although it is not remunerated, the trainee enjoys full social security cover and can also apply for *ACCRE* and *EDEN*. The trainee also knows that they are not obliged to start a business if the test period suggests that their business idea is not going to be viable. For further details write to Union des Couveuses, 14 rue Delambre, 75014 Paris or email contact@uniondescouveuses.com.

DJA funds

These are state and European Union funds for people under 40 years of age, with previous farming experience, who are prepared to take a farm management course to help their dream of running their own farm. UK farmers with previous experience wishing to plunge into vineyards ripe for redevelopment should take note of these available funds. Contact the local Chambre d'Agriculture or visit www.adasea.net – the farmer *départemental* federation.

FISAC (fonds d'intervention pour les services, l'artisanat et le commerce)

This is a state grant assisting the creation of a new shop, service or artisan's business serving a small community with a population of under 2,000. Villagers crying out for a local bar or a concentration of anglophiles wanting a pub are examples. Tourist businesses such as camping sites, hotels and restaurants are non-starters. Chambers of commerce or the *DRCA* (*délégation régionale au commerce et à l'artisanat*) should be contacted.

FRAC (fonds regionaux d'aide au conseil)

Contact the prefecture or chamber of commerce to see if this aid is available. They grant funds, up to a generous limit of around

31,000€, representing between 50 and 80 per cent of the cost of professional market surveys and business development plans if the future entrepreneur needs to have these prepared by specialists. The latter must be officially approved companies (*conventionnés*). Foreigners with a sound, ambitious project should take advantage of this.

Employees who want to start a business

If you are employed with a French company, employment law provides employees with two practical possibilities of investigating or putting into practice a business idea. In both cases the risk-taking factor of business creation is greatly reduced as the employee can regain their previous job if they decide after all not to become a business or remain self-employed. In practice the possibilities described below are most likely to apply to employees who have been with a large (national or multi-national) company for many years.

Le congé pour création d'entreprise
Like a sabbatical period this allows for a year off to study or start a project. Two years employment – not necessarily continuous – with the same company or group of companies is a basic condition for this *congé*. Unless the employer is outstandingly generous no salary will be paid during this period, and only a relatively small part of the missing salary can be accumulated by not taking the fifth week of holiday, to which employees are entitled every year, for the six years immediately preceding the *congé* year. Pre-planning, and well in advance, and personal savings are crucial. With the possibility at some companies of working up to 220 hours a year over the legal limit of 35 hours a week it may be

possible to build up extra time which can be carried forward through the years to help fund the *congé* year.

Bear in mind that benefits built up under the terms of an employment contract cannot be added to during this year's absence and the employee cannot return to their company before the year is up. They can however give their employer two months' official notice, before the period expires, if they need or wish to extend the test for another year. People who really can't make up their minds can have another *congé pour création* three years after the first one!

If during this period the project looks sound or the business is performing well they will need to come to a decision three months before the year is up as their employer must have three months' notice by recorded-delivery letter of their intention to leave the company. If, on the other hand, they wish to rejoin their company the employer must also be informed officially three months before the year is up.

Key staff may be refused the *congé* request in companies employing under 200 people, although this decision can be contested. The start date for the period requested may also be delayed for up to six months and there are also different quota conditions depending on whether companies employ more or less than 200 people. Managements of very small, small- and medium-sized companies (*TPE, PME/PMI*) will have strong arguments for refusing the request.

Temps partiel pour création d'entreprise
In many respects this part-time employment possibility is an easier solution for the employee who wants to try out his project,

although their employer may find it difficult to dovetail the work of two part-time employees if another (new) part-time employee is required to make up productivity.

Employment law stipulates the same conditions as those for the *congé pour création d'entreprise*. The amount of part-time work requested must also be stipulated and, as with the *congé pour création d'entreprise* possibility, the nature of the new business project must be revealed. (Since August 2003 the law has allowed for restrictive exclusivity clauses in employment contracts, with the exception of those for salaried exclusive representatives, to be waived for these *congé* and *temps partiel* periods: provided the employee does not ruin or try to ruin his employer's business by poaching the employer's customers.)

If the employer accepts the request, the employment contract must be modified to show the new reduced salary, job description – if there are any changes – and exactly when the reduced hours of work will be worked. If the employer refuses the reduced hours of work request, they must explain why in their official letter notifying the decision. This decision can be contested by contacting the local industrial tribunal (*conseil de prud'hommes*) within 15 days of receiving notification. NB: employees should not miss the opportunity that all salaried people have to vote every five years in the election of employers and salaried employees who make up the members of these tribunals.

Employees are paid in accordance with the reduced number of hours and cannot resume their full-time employment, if they so wish, before the year expires. They will then be paid not less than their previous salary.

Exemption from payment of social security contributions applies to an income figure up to 120 per cent of the national basic minimum salary for the first 12 months of any new business, but is subject to the following conditions and limitations:

- at least 910 hours of salaried employment during the 12 months immediately preceding the business start date; (approximately six months on the basis of a 35 hour week);
- *and* at least 455 hours of salaried employment (around three months) during the first 12 months immediately following this start date.

Despite the fact that 20 per cent of France's work force are in the French civil service, administrative systems will not automatically recognise and award this entitlement. Exemption must be applied for to the appropriate social security contributions collection agency (*URSSAF* or other) within the 12-month period and at least 90 days after the new business start date. For further information visit www.urssaf.fr.

It is vital that the procedure laid down for notifying the employer is strictly followed. Not least to ensure that the employee effectively retains his employment status during the *congé pour création d'enterprise* option and can benefit from the above exemption. *DDTEFP* offices can supply the full official text governing the above possibilities.

Note also that if the business fails or is wound up the right to unemployment benefit as a previous salaried employee will only apply if application is made within three years of having terminated the last salaried employment contract. This highlights once again the importance of the first three years' results in new businesses.

Unemployed people who want to start a business

To encourage new business creations the national employment agency (*ANPE*) offers a free consultancy service and financial advantages for the registered unemployed.

The consultancy service (*EPCE* (*évaluation préalable à la création ou à la reprise d'entreprise*)) examines the strengths and weaknesses of the project, weighs up its practicability and sets out the (theoretical) ways and means of setting up in business and achieving success by drawing up a formal plan showing what to do and when. In practice, a professional consultant discusses with the new-business candidate their personal and employment background to see if they have the necessary knowledge of their project's market situation and the commercial, technical, management and financial aptitudes to make a go of it.

Once the business has started, if income is less than 70 per cent of previous salary on which unemployment benefit (*allocations d'ASSEDIC*) has been calculated, part of the difference will continue to be paid as benefit for a maximum period of 18 months. Unemployed people over 50 years old obtain better advantages.

As with salaried employees starting a business, if, despite all preparatory studies, the business fails within three years, unemployment benefit is obtained. Risk-taking is therefore reduced.

And also, as with salaried employees starting a business, the same exemption and conditions apply to social security contributions in relation to income. Periods of unemployment *with* paid benefit count as 'salaried employment' for these purposes on the basis of one day's unemployment being equivalent to 6 hours' salaried employment. The unemployed are obviously deemed to start their day later!

EUROPEAN UNION GRANTS

While various EU schemes exist for small- and medium-sized businesses note that applications are only received for considera-tion once a year before certain dates – and sometimes only every few years – and that obtaining a decision and payment of any grant is a lengthy process.

What schemes exist and how are applications made?

The European Commission manages funds which are awarded with particularly favourable consideration given to any of the fol-lowing points:

◆ Will the project create employment?
◆ Does it reduce environmental pollution or improve the local environment?
◆ Does it help people fulfil their potential or enhance human rela-tions through new cultural establishments (theatre groups and dance schools for example) or by providing further education or training courses (a management course linked to business English for example)?
◆ Does it break new research or technological ground and involve at least two EU member countries?

All projects must be truly European, by involving at least three other EU members as partners or by providing a European service which is advantageous to at least one other member country. Contact the *cellule Entreprises* which handles applications for France at the European Commission in Brussels.

Other grants (*les aides indirectes*) are managed jointly by individual member states and the European Commission, with the latter taking the final decision after an initial selection by the former. These grants come from the *FEOGA* (European funds for agriculture) to develop rural areas and from the *FEDER* (European funds for regional development) to develop regional industry.

Free advice and information are provided by the Euro Info Centre, in the Paris Chamber of Commerce, 27, avenue de Friedland, 75000 Paris. It will indicate the appropriate EU scheme for projects. For further information visit www.ccip.fr/eic.

The European Business Network based in Brussels, with offices throughout Europe, is also a useful contact. It is quite independent of the European Commission and acts as an information exchange for entrepreneurs seeking business development advice, European funds or partners. Visit the English website www. csreurope.org.

LOANS (AND CONSULTANCY)
EDEN (encouragement au développement d'entreprises nouvelles)

This state measure giving financial aid and professional advice for the 'encouragement and development of new businesses' will particularly interest foreigners who are going to be awarded a *CAPE* entitlement (see page 77) or are among the registered unemployed who are 50 years old or more. It also applies to single parents, widows receiving benefit and people with extremely limited means, and also people under 30 years old who meet certain conditions.

If awarded, it provides an interest-free loan with a maximum repayment period of five years on the following (2005) sliding scale:

◆ not more than 6,098€ for a sole trader;
◆ not more than 9,145€ if more than one applicant for the same project.

Also providing that, in both cases, a complementary loan which amounts to at least 50 per cent of the state loan is obtained from another (approved) source.

Additionally, *chéques EDEN* – similar to the *conseils-chéquier* device – are provided which are exchanged for up to 35 hours' time with a business consultant for management, development and marketing advice etc. over the first three years. As a sensible monitoring tool an hour a month's consultancy is logical. Approximately 60€ of the consultant's set hourly fee (75€ in 2005) is paid by the state.

The 12-month exemption from social security payments under the *ACCRE* system applies. And as with *ACCRE* a fully and correctly completed application form must be deposited before the business starts. Contact the local *DDTEFP* for details of organisations that handle loan applications.

France Initiative Réseau (FIR)

The principal objective of this national association with around 250 local offices known as *PFILs* (*plates-formes d'initiatives locales*) is to obtain funds for no-interest, no-guarantee loans (*prêts d'honneur*) in a financial bracket ranging from as little as 1,500€ to 38,000€. Other types of loans, such as *EDEN*, may be obtained through *PFILs* which also provide advice for up to two years for new businesses. *FIR* is a possibility for projects, for example, that are not selected by *Réseau entreprendre* (see page 89) and many *micro entreprises* (see Taxation in Chapter 3).The very small enterprises group (*TPEs*) fall into this category. Write to France Initiative Réseau, 14, rue Delambre, 75014 Paris or see www.fir.asso.fr.

ADIE (association pour le droit à l'initiative économique)

This association is represented in over half of France's *départements* and provides low-interest loans and advice over a 24 month period for small business projects which will probably remain cottage industries (*micro entreprises*). Every year thousands of new businesses are thankful to them. Difficult financial circumstances need to be shown. People who for one legitimate reason or another have been refused bank loans can apply for small loans, up to 5,000€, provided their application is backed by a third-party guarantee (*caution solidaire*) for 50 per cent of the loan amount.

The *ADIE* loan can be combined with another loan such as *EDEN* so that a more substantial initial fund is available and *ADIE* may be able to supply small, but essential equipment on a loan basis ranging from professional hair-drying equipment for home-visit hairdressers to photographic equipment for photographers. Decisions and release of funds are quick and the association caters for a wide range of applicants: from architects just starting up, to glass-blowers and market stallholders.

Write to ADIE, 4, boulevard Poissonnière, 75009 Paris or see www.adie.org.

RACINES

These are local funds reserved exclusively for low-interest loans to enterprising women, such as boutique owners, hairdressers, etc. Write to RACINES, 8 square de la Dordogne, 75017 Paris or visit www.racines-clefe.com.

FGIF (Fonds de Garantie à L'Initiative des Femmes)

FGIF helps enterprising women, by guaranteeing up to 70 per cent of bank loans for new businesses. The maximum amount guaranteed is 38,000€ (2005 rate) and the minimum 5,000€. This service will be provided for a fee as a percentage of the guaranteed amount. Single women, such as those who wish to be completely independent in their business affairs, or those who are fed up with not being paid the same as their male colleagues for doing the same job (teachers excepted) although by law they should be, will find this a useful incentive. This will also be of interest to women with children at school who want to organise their own work so that they are with their children during the Wednesday break from school. The funds can also be used to aid business development during the first five years. All women, regardless of age and personal employment situation, and all types of activities and business structures, including businesses operating from home, are eligible.

Apply to the *Missions départementales des droits de la femme* in prefectures or write to FGIF, 10–12, rue des trois Fontanot, 92000 Nanterre.

Equal opportunity for the sexes is the law, but in practice women are excluded from certain jobs and this is one important reason why women open their own businesses. Reports concur that women are generally good at PR, cultivating good customer relationships and therefore customer loyalty. Although plenty of women *and* men have hairdressing salons for women in France you will almost never find a man running a perfume shop. (Interestingly, some of the best perfume creators who literally sniff out new fragrances for the latest products are men.)

Services provided at home for people, including door-to-door transport, are a big growth area and, apart from garden-maintenance, are dominated by women.

Réseau entreprendre
This is a network of 31 area associations designed to help future small- and medium-sized businesses (*PME*), but not businesses that intend to remain one-man bands, by awarding a no-interest, no-guarantee loan (*prêt d'honneur*) and by offering free consultations with a team of professional people: working or retired businessmen, bankers, legal experts, etc. These are people who can give sound advice and possibly put forward alternative proposals or modifications based on their fields of expertise.

Hand-written motivation letters accompanied by a CV accentuating employment experience and skills which relate particularly to the project should accompany a business development plan or details of the project, for initial appraisal. The project will then be filtered and discussed before a definite commitment is made to help the entrepreneur on a one-to-one consultancy basis through the start-up period and initial years. As the members of the association put up the money for the loans themselves they only accept cases where motivation and the project are outstanding. (Note that if the business does fail the outstanding loan amount is written off.)

The website details are: www.reseau-entreprendre.org. This association will only normally consider projects with projected setting-up costs (*bilan de départ actif*) in the 80,000 to 500,000€ bracket, and offers loans up to approximately 46,000€.

Réseau entreprendre en France

This is a federation, organised by Chambers of Commerce with supportive banks throughout France, that issues certificates of approval (*Passeport Entreprendre*) for new projects which satisfy their professional consultants. The *Passeports* are an indication to *réseau* member organisations that they can consider offering security for bank loans.

Contact the Espace Entreprendre in Chambers of Commerce or visit www.entreprendre-en-France.fr.

REGIONAL LOANS
Prêt régional aux créateurs d'entreprises

This regional development loan is not available in all regions and Chambers of Commerce or Trade (*métiers*) will have up-to-date information. Designed for new industrial and small-scale (*artisanal*) manufacturers, it offers a no-interest loan without any guarantee, repayable, in certain regions, over seven years. Regional authorities granting the loan will look for a good balance between personal (company) funds and existing bank loan(s), so that the regional loan will be a complementary, albeit important, source of finance. Loan brackets vary: for example, Provence, Alpes and the Côtes d'Azur region in 2005 considered loans between 15,000 and 75,000€.

This loan should not be confused with *PRCE* which is a regional development grant for companies under one year old who intend taking on new permanent staff. Like the regional development loan, it is only available in certain regions.

USEFUL REGIONAL AND *DÉPARTEMENTAL* ADDRESSES AND WEBSITES

Cantal Expansion, 16–18 rue Paul Doumer, 15015 Aurillac cedex.
www.cybercantal.org
Awards annually about 50 interest free four-year loans. All new businesses are considered.

Ardab,19, rue Colson, 21000 Dijon
The Burgundy regional association for artisan industry development. No-interest loans between 30 to 50 per cent of the investment amount are considered.

There are two useful information agents in the Franche-Comté region:

Cré-Entreprendre, ZA les prés de Vaux, 25000 Besancon
Départemental loans from 1,500 to 15,000€ which may be under-
written by the SOFARIS organisation (see also *PCE* loans in
Chapter 6). The loan comes with ongoing advice.

Vivre en Bresse, Grande rue de la Bresse, 39230 Chaumergy
Smaller interest free loans, of up to 20 per cent of the investment
amount and not more than 7,500€.

Fondation Crédit mutuel, 46, rue du Port-Boyer, 44000 Nantes
Interest free loans for businesses with original products and
which also create local employment. They provide around 70
loans a year. The Fondation's operating area includes the
Limousin region which is increasingly popular with British property buyers. Nantes itself is considered to be one of the most
attractive areas in which to live and work in France.

Fondation Crédit mutuel Océan, 34, rue Léandre-Merlet, 85000
La-roche-sur-Yon
Original business projects in the Vendée, Charente-Maritime and
Deux-Sèvres *départements* may be granted a 7,600€, interest free
five-year loan requiring no guarantee. In comparison to the
Nantes Fondation, only around ten loans are provided annually.

USEFUL VOCABULARY

allocations d'ASSEDIC	unemployment benefit
caution solidaire	guarantee provided by third party
conseil de prud'hommes	industrial tribunal
couveuse	organisation supervising future entrepreneur
prêts d'honneur	interest free loans requiring no guarantee
société conventionnée	officially approved supplier or service company

6

Private funds, bank loans, venture capital and leasing

Official loans, grants and subsidies will usually be accorded only if the entrepreneur shows they have obtained, are going to obtain or have at least tried to obtain other funds from personal/private and commercial sources.

PRIVATE FUNDS

Depending on the business structure selected and the protection it offers personal estate, the entrepreneur should calculate how much of their own money they are prepared to invest, and possibly lose, if the business is unsuccessful. Family, friends, associates and banks will need to have proof of personal commitment before risking their funds. Banks (see page 96) will normally look for at least 30 per cent of initial funds coming from private sources before considering a loan.

Entrepreneurs in France in the under-30 age group on average invest under 7,500€ from personal sources in new businesses, while the over-30 age group invest on average around 15,000€. Three out of four new businesses in France start up thanks to gifts and loans from family and close friends. Formal agreements should, of course, be drawn up stating amounts invested, plus repayment and dividend conditions, and registered with the tax office before the 15th of February of the following year so that the funds are not considered as income.

Since 2005, family gifts of up to 30,000€ to help start a new business – and also to help buy an existing business – are exempt from gift tax. (Buyers of businesses also qualify for a reduction on *IR* tax of up to 5,000€ a year.) And anyone (*personne physique*) investing in a new company which is not on the stock exchange benefits from 25 per cent tax relief on the amount invested, up to an investment amount of approximately 20,000€. If the company fails within the first eight years, investors may also be entitled to deduct the amount lost from their income returns to the tax authorities. The tax office will confirm the exact maximum limits allowed. Married couples are entitled to twice the single person allowances.

Below are outlined some of the various savings plans that exist which can help finance business creations.

Le livret d'épargne d'entreprise (LEE)

This plan runs from two to five years and a reduced rate loan, which is *not* automatically agreed, may be taken out against it for a two- to 15-year period. Not all banks propose this plan and you should bear this in mind if a bank account in France is being opened for the first time. A minimum initial deposit of 750€ is necessary followed by regular amounts totalling at least 540€ a year during the plan's life. The limit to total savings is 45,800€ and interest is attracted at a rate of around 5 per cent tax-free. Withdrawals can now be made before the two-year period is reached provided the funds are used within six months to help finance a new business being created by the plan holder or a member of his immediate family.

Le plan d'épargne en actions (PEA)

Withdrawals from this stock portfolio investment plan, which was originally designed as a personal investment plan of at least eight years, can now be made, tax-free, before five years are up to help finance a new business. The funds must be deposited in a bank account for the business within three months.

Le plan d'épargne logement (PEL)

This is the equivalent of a building society's savings plan, and it can now be used to buy business premises provided that they are also going to be the plan holder's main home.

BANKS

Shopping around for bank loans is recommended. It doesn't follow that the bank that has been used for personal loans for domestic or property purchases (*prêts à la consommation* or *prêts immobiliers*) and manages your personal account will offer loans to help start a small- or medium-sized business. A useful website is www.FinancePME.com as it provides a free service (the banks sponsor the website) to find the most advantageous loan deal for new businesses, according to individual circumstances and requirements. Large banks are more interested in big business, and if they are ready to consider a loan may take a long time to decide. (Barclays Bank, for example, have been in France for nearly a century now, and offer mortgages, personal banking and stock exchange investment services, but they do not solicit the small-business loans market.) A local bank that already knows the entrepreneur and can be easily visited to build up a long-term relationship is the ideal solution. Most banks with local offices will have a separate division for entrepreneurs, and standard banking conditions for *entrepreneurs* and *professionnels* setting up as *EI*s. Although interviews will usually be by appointment it is worth checking banking hours when shopping around. The 35-hour week means that many banks are closed on Mondays or on Saturday afternoons or that experienced staff, who are familiar with the area's business environment, may have some time off during the week.

Standard banking conditions will include charges for:

- overdrafts, to cover cash-flow problems *after* the first 12 months and not to provide initial finance. Overdrafts must be agreed in advance;
- commission for crediting accounts immediately with the value of a customer's draft (*traite*) with a payment date of up to 90 days, although any unsettled invoices corresponding to drafts still remain the account holder's risk. This is not the same as using a factoring company which takes over non-payment risk;
- cheque negotiation fees for non-euro cheques.

They should not include charges for writing out cheques and for cash deposits and withdrawals as a mutual agreement between banks for these free-banking services was drawn up in 2004. However, it is worth checking this if a new bank account is being opened as not all banks respect this agreement.

Classic bank loans are medium- to long-term. Banks will require firm personal guarantees to cover loans, especially if no guarantees are provided by any state or regional-development aid.

Guarantees may be a charge against business material and equipment, property, personal estate or a third-party who signs an *acte de caution.*

The principal bank loans available are outlined below.

Les prêts bancaires aux entreprises (prêts CODEVI)

These medium- to long-term loans cost around five per cent and are available, subject to a favourable decision, to all *PME* businesses with a turnover not exceeding 76,000,000€.

Le prêt à la création d'entreprise (PCE)

No collateral is required for this loan which may be granted to new businesses or businesses under three years' old and companies with private shareholders that employ no more than 10 people. It is aimed at small projects as the loan ranges from 2,000 to a maximum of 7,000€. It is for a fixed five-year period, with the first of 54 monthly repayments starting after six months into the loan. The interest rate is around 6 per cent. No *existing* or *previous* bank loans must have been agreed for the business project, but a medium- to long-term bank loan must be established to accompany it. The bank loan must be between two to three times the *PCE* amount. The *banque de développement des petites et moyennes entreprises* (*BDPME*) which provides finance for small- and medium-sized businesses issues these loans and can also underwrite other bank loans. Visit their website www.bdpme.fr for full details and conditions.

Les prêts bonifiés à l'artisanat

Any business registered at a *Chambre des Métiers* is entitled to apply for this 'improvement' loan, from a bank, such as the Banque Populaire, BNP, Crédit Agricole, Crédit Mutuel, Crédit Lyonnais and Société Générale, for installation or improvement of equipment bringing it into line with safety, hygiene and environmental regulations. The interest rate is around 6 per cent for a loan of not more than 46,000€, representing up to 80 per cent HT of the cost. HT is the amount exclusive of VAT (TVA). Loans are between two and 15 years and come from state funds allocated to the banks which decide if loan applications meet the required conditions.

VENTURE CAPITAL

Commercial organisations providing venture capital and minor shareholdings – not to be confused with major shareholders helping the long-term development of the business – will be looking for businesses with outstanding rapid development potential so that funds invested will have maximum return over the shortest possible period.

National organisations are only interested in large projects and, in particular, those which break new technological ground or offer a quite revolutionary product. Any project, asking for less than 150,000€ venture capital is unlikely to even be considered. There are also *regional* organisations (*Sociétés de développement regional (SDR)*), geared to investing funds in projects which must have a regional interest, for example a new private transport service for the regional community. Here again only large projects will be considered, seeking at least 75,000€ venture capital.

Local organisations, however, exist in certain areas which may provide venture capital upwards from 7,500€ for new small- and medium-sized businesses of all types, with industry and services to businesses more likely to attract investment than new technology businesses. The local Chamber of Commerce should have an up-to-date list. For the Paris area, a useful starting point is the Ile-de-France Développement website: www.idfd.fr.

Venture capital 'clubs' have a different philosophy. They consist of small groups of individuals who want to make a social statement by investing in small businesses providing a product or service in the local community's interest or promising to provide some local employment. As with any venture-capital investor the project will be carefully studied, especially as investors will be risking their own money. Investments are usually made for about five years for amounts between 1,500 and 5,000€. One of the main chain of clubs is *CIGALES* (*clubs d'investisseurs pour une gestion alternative et locale de l'épargne*). Visit www.cigales.asso.fr for more information on their approximately 80 branches throughout France. Note that applications should in the first instance be addressed to the federation's head office: *CIGALES*, 61, rue Victor Hugo, 93500 Pantin.

Moving up the 'club' ladder in investment amounts is the association *Fédération Love Money* which has an estimated 20 branches. Each branch is a non-profit-making *association* subject to the 1901 law (*loi 1901*) setting out *association* rules and regulations. They collect individual members' contributions which total not less than 50,000€ as investment capital in an *SA* company. (*SAs* – see Chapter 3 – must have at least 37,000€ capital.) All business projects, seeking sufficient capital can be considered. The Federation's *Love* is altruistic as the association's are non-profit making. Consult www.lovemoney.org for full details in English.

Business angels are exactly what they suggest: 'heaven-sent' private investors, who are probably retired or previous entrepreneurs, looking to invest in and give some of their spare time to help new small businesses. The number of *angels* is growing fast in France, although still a long way behind the UK. Investors are encouraged by certain tax-deductible allowances on their investments in company structures provided that they (the investors) have set themselves up officially as an individual venture capital business (*société unipersonnnelle à risqué* (*SUIR*)) and invest in industrial, commercial or artisan company structures. New companies in these sorts of businesses and looking for investment funds of around 7,500€ should visit www.franceangels.org.

LEASING (*CRÉDIT-BAIL*)

Often used for acquiring business, and private, vehicles on a hire basis, with an option to buy for a small residual amount at the end of the contract, leasing can also be used to buy business premises (over a certain value) or capital equipment. No initial outlay is required. In the case of property, moreover, loans (*crédit-bail immobilier*) can be up to 20 years if required, a period rarely accorded by banks. All lease repayments are tax-deductible.

Particular points and clauses to watch out for in this form of contract are:

- Does the contract provide options to continue leasing the same material at a reduced rate or to return it, as well as the option-to-buy upon completion of the lease agreement?
- If the business fails during the period of contract, would the supplier (the finance house, as they actually own the material) recover it and cancel the contract?
- Is the monthly repayment amount fixed or degressive? (It should certainly not increase.)
- Does the contract call for a personal guarantee? Consider taking out insurance to cover this, instead of jeopardising personal property.

The customer copy of the contract application form should also contain a seven-day cancellation period possibility which must be signed and sent off within that period if there is a change of heart.

USEFUL VOCABULARY

acte de caution	(signed) guarantee for loan
avale	signed acceptance of a draft
capital-risque	venture capital
découvert	overdraft
mise de fonds initiale	seed money
prêt à la consommation	bank loan for non-business purposes
traite	draft with payment date

USEFUL ADDRESSES AND WEBSITES

L'association nationale de capitale de proximité
ANCP-Epicea, 7, rue Domrémy, 75013 Paris
Visit www.eficea.org
Publishes a guide to all organisations offering finance to businesses operating locally.

L'association française des investisseurs en capital
AFIC, 14, rue de Berri, 75008 Paris.
Visit www.afic.asso.fr
The association of capital investment organisations.

L'Union nationale des investisseurs en capital pour les entreprises régionales
Visit www.unicer.asso.fr
National group of venture capital companies which invest in regional developing companies.

Premises

An important factor to be borne in mind when choosing the type of premises is that the *domiciliation de l'entreprise* – the business' head office address – does not necessarily have to be the place where the actual activity (*lieu d'exercice de l'activité*) is carried out. In the case of an *entreprise individuelle* no registered head office is required, and their business address (*adresse entreprise*) can well be their home address. Especially if all the productive work is carried out away from the business' home address and customers have no need to visit the business' premises.

Do you want to buy premises outright or rent on a long- or short-term basis? Would it make sense to operate from home (regulations permitting) extending your property or using or converting part of it? Under what circumstances would it be sensible to register the business' head office permanently at a local *Centre de domiciliation*? What are the advantages of taking limited office space in a local *Centre d'affaires*? If there is a *zone franche* (tax-free zone) locally, what are the real advantages? Before registering the business a choice must be made, which will depend on the type of business and its requirements, and the initial resources available.

BUYING PREMISES

The buying procedure – described on page 110 – is the same as for residential property purchase, whether you find the premises and negotiate the purchase through an estate agent or a specialised *consultant en immobilier d'entreprise* or deal directly (*particulier à particulier*) with the seller. The latter is only recommended for those who have already purchased premises in France successfully without going through an agent.

Particular attention should be paid to net floor areas which are usually expressed as an overall surface area, in metres of course, without necessarily giving the dimensions. If an on-plan purchase is being made and there is no show unit around the same size to visit look at other existing units around the same size. The Carrez Law stipulates that surface areas for units within a multi-unit block, whether they are offices, shops or warehouses or depots, given on official documents must be correct to within 5 per cent either side. An *indépendent* (detached) building is not subject to the *Loi Carrez*. If you are buying a detached building on its own plot of land check whether the planning permission density for the plot (*coefficient d'occupation des sols* (*COS*)) is up to its limit or not. An expanding business may need more space later on.

If further planning permission is possible an official application for approval of any work extending the premises by more than 20 m² has to be lodged with the town hall or the local office of the *Direction Départementale de l'Equipement* (*DDE*). An official application form for *permis de construire* (*PC*) must be used and the laid-down procedure strictly followed. Any changes to windows and business signs or building work providing less than an additional 20 m² (subject to planning permission density limits) must simply be notified to either of the above authorities using an official *déclaration de travaux* form following the laid-down notification (*déclaration*) procedure.

While residential property has to cover at least 16 m² net floor area overall, business premises and offices of all types are not subject to a minimum overall floor area or minimum room sizes. However, two office-based persons who both receive customers or clients would be cramped in a 16 m² space. Thirty m², equivalent to a medium-sized through-lounge-living room, would be about right. If a number of staff are employed, for example in a telephone-canvassing business, where there are no customers visiting, less space per person would be required: around 4 m² per person would be ideal with cubicle partitioning. Note that businesses employing more than 25 people must provide a refectory area, which should be away from the work area if staff request it.

Due attention should be paid to the type of business activity permitted in the premises. A *local commercial* in a shopping mall (*centre commercial*) can only be used for shops, boutiques, banks or service businesses. An industrial or trading estate (*zone industrielle* or *zone d'activités*) just nearby may well have a large workshop/warehouse building with mezzanine office area ideal for a variety of manufacturing/repair/wholesale/ex-factory sales activities. Note that any new retail business with a sales area of more than 300 m² requires prior approval from the *Préfecture*. (This regulation was introduced some years ago to protect the old corner shop, which offered a useful service, from the ever-increasing competition from new supermarkets and hypermarkets.) Approval appears to be given readily, however, to new discount-supermarkets with over 300 m² sales area. They open up all the time providing fierce competition, in turn, to classic supermarkets and hypermarkets. *Parc tertiares* are modern office block estates which may accept some quiet high-tech industry or light engineering. Check whether there is any clause allowing or prohibiting directly competitive businesses in the same building. This is particularly relevant to retail businesses, with good frontages, where passing trade is important.

All properties must be certified free of asbestos (*amiante*) or with asbestos dust giving off less than five fibres of asbestos per litre of air; and any accessible lead-content paint (*peintures au plomb*). They must also show, if in an officially recognised termite area, if termites are present or not (*l'état parasitique*). Additionally all properties for sale (or for let) must now indicate a list of possible natural or techno-logical local risks such as flooding, earthquakes, pollution, etc. if they are in an officially deemed risk-area. If no indication is included with the contract ask for confirmation from the *Préfecture* that the area is not a risk-area. An estimated five million people in France live in what are now known to be flood-risk areas.

If planning permission is given for transformation of, say, an old barn with some lighting to a modern warehouse with an office area, the insulation and electrical-wiring system will almost cer-tainly need improvement. The CONSUEL organisation (www.consuel.com) will visit the premises, at a charge, to con-firm whether or not the installation complies with current requirements.

Individual units for sale in modern office blocks are rare as the economics of office developments is based on rental income. Converted town centre buildings are a better source. An estate agent's advertisement, in the local paper under *Immobilier*, *Entreprises et Commerces* or a property owner's advertisement in a national magazine such as *Les Annonces Immobilières entre particuliers* might read:

A vendre

Murs commerciaux (business premises). *centre ville, emplacement 1ère ordre. Local 60 m². tout équipé. Vitrine (anti-effraction). Accueil, coffre fort, 2 bureaux, WC, local technique* (boiler room, mains). *locaux équipés avec climatisation* (air-conditioned). *Ancienne agence assurance. Plusieurs possibilités. Prix_____*

The translated words in brackets would not of course be in the advertisement.

Larger units, either individual buildings or premises in a row of buildings in an out-of-town industrial/trading estate can be found through national specialists in larger offices, depots and industrial units, such as DTZ Jean Thouard. An advertisement for the sale of part of an industrial building with a mezzanine office might read:

A vendre   295 m²

Dans la ZI, une partie d'un atelier d'un bâtiment industriel à usage d'atelier, avec 70 m² de bureau en mezzanine. Grande hauteur sous toit avec proximité de l'autoroute. Disponibilité et prix: nous consulter.

An advertisement offering units for rent in the last phase of a new office block development might read :

A louer   50, 80 et 150 m²

Dans la dernière tranche du Parc Tertiaire 'New Business', il reste quelques lots de bureaux neufs, cloisonnés et climatisés. Access direct à partir de l'autoroute. Disponibilité: immédiate.

An advertisement for an old town centre building, in a prime position, might offer three modernised office floors with a lift, for sale, or possibly for rent, as follows:

A vendre   *1100m² divisibles (could be split into units)*

Au coeur du centre ville, sur la meilleure portion du boulevard. Trois plateaux de bureaux (3ème, 4ème et 5ème étages). Ascenseur. Locaux refaits à neuf, climatisés. Disponibiilté: 2ème trimestre 2006.

Notaires publics (see *acte de vente* on page 110), who are all appointed by the French government, can also act as property agents. The main advantage is that their negotiating fee, which they do not like to be called 'commission', is laid down by a national sliding scale related to the price of the sale.

Chambers of commerce may also have details of available premises, although their 'for sale' information sheets usually offer premises (*murs*) *and* the existing business (*fonds de commerce*) as an overall proposition.

Placing a business-premises search advertisement in the local press under *Locaux Commerciaux* and *Achats* can have a good response as proprietors and estate agents sometimes have the misconceived idea that they will get a better price by selling to a foreigner who, supposedly, has not checked out property values in the area. The advertisement should start along the lines:

'homme d'affaires étranger recherche'

before proceeding to the location and size and type of premises sought.

The buying procedure

Two preliminary sales contracts are possible after the verbal or written offer (*offre d'achat*) has been accepted:

+ the *compromis de vente*
+ or the *promesse unilatérale de vente*

Both contracts specify the precise address of the property and its total usable space with a brief description (such as the number of rooms with surface areas), the land and any other local property taxes, the agent's commission or *notaires* negotiating fee, completion and possession dates. It is important at this point to detail fixtures, fittings and any permanent office equipment which will remain part of the property. Note that a *notaires* negotiating fee should not be confused with legal fees. Notaries sometimes advertise premises with an all inclusive *acte de vente en main* price: the price for the seller plus the negotiating and legal fees.

Both contracts ask for immediate deposits, held in a sequestered account, of up to 10 per cent of the purchase price.

The *compromis* contract is the contract more frequently used. Estate agents are quite accustomed to drawing up these preliminary contracts. If you are dealing directly with the property's owner you are advised to have the preliminary contract drawn up and signed before a notary and preferably the one who will draw up the *acte authentique*. Deferment clauses (*conditions suspensives*) should be included making the purchase subject to any required finance being obtained – it is advisable to detail the nature of the loan and the organisation concerned – and null and void if a local town planning decision is revealed which will depreciate the value of the property. The buyer's deposit is returned in these instances. A *droit de préemption* clause will also ensure that, in the event of a compulsory purchase order before completion which precludes the sale, the buyer recovers their deposit.

The *unilatérale* contract does not commit the buyer to purchase the property whereas the seller is bound to reserve the property for the potential buyer at an agreed price for an agreed period of time. As with the *compromis* contract, *conditions suspensives* and a *droit de préemption* clause should be included. The buyer's deposit is returnable if these clauses have to be applied.

Bilingual assistance from a qualified person is strongly recommended when signing agreements to documents as these will usually only be in French. Don't expect any special assistance from the notary, who as the French government's appointee must be French and is unlikely therefore to be truly bilingual. You can appoint your own notary, but if it is agreed to use only one notary the choice is the property owner's privilege.

Please note the following:

- A seven-day cooling-off period gives the buyer additional protection at this stage. Buyers can change their minds, no questions asked, within seven days of signing a preliminary contract.
- During the agreed period prior to the *acte de vente définitive* the notary verifies property title, outstanding loans, charges,

obtains the asbestos, termite and lead-free paint certificates (if they have not already been produced) and checks land registry details and town planning regulations, and any other local regulations which may concern the property.

◆ The completion deed reconfirms the information given in the preliminary contract, with more detailed information on the property, with the exclusion now of any previous *suspensive/préemption* clauses.

◆ Details of notary fees, i.e. legal fees, can be consulted under '*frais de notaires*' on the notaries' website: www.immonot.com.

◆ Buying business premises offers certain financial advantages. Transfer tax, notarial fees and land tax (*taxe foncière*) are tax-deductible company expenses. If the premises are a personal purchase by the owner of the business they can be let to the company for a rent which can cover any mortgage repayments. Additionally, the premises remain part of the personal estate of their owner and cannot be possessed or impounded, unless the business is an *entreprise individuelle* (where there is no distinction between private and business resources) if the company fails.

Prices

So many variables are involved that it is meaningless to give examples of new, old or renovated office, industrial and warehouse prices throughout France for comparative purposes.

Apart from looking at advertisements for business premises *(locaux commerciaux* and *locaux professionnels*) in newspapers, look at the following magazines and/or website:

Logic-Immo magazine. Distributed free outside many bars, petrol stations, bakers etc. Consult the *Immobilier Divers* pages for further information.
www.logic-immo.com. English instructions for property search for further information. The website has some colour photos (enlargeable) and descriptions in English.

Entre Particuliers magazine. There are no agents. You should consult the colour sections and the special *Locaux* section for further information.
Use the www.entreparticuliers.com website property search service.

www.bureaux-commerces.com has information/descriptions in French.
www.cession-commerce.com has information/descriptions in French, plus photos.
Both of the above are particularly easy to visit and use.

Visit www.dtz.com or www.dtzresearch.com for industrial or commercial property search.

If you are looking for a home which will also be used, or partially converted, as business premises (see page 121, Working from home) the French notaries website www.immoprix.com is also useful. It shows average transaction prices i.e. 'sold' prices, throughout France for old and new properties and also for building land. Use of all private property or construction possibilities for business purposes must, of course, be verified with the local planning department before purchase.

USEFUL VOCABULARY

accueil	reception area
atelier	workshop
centre commercial	shopping centre/mall
COS	planning permission density
local commercial	business premises (shops, offices, depots, factories, etc.)
murs commerciaux	business premises (for sale)
parc tertiaire	service businesses' estate
PC	planning permission
technopôle	science and technology (research/laboratory) estate
vente – particulier à particulier	private sale, without any agent
zone d'activités (ZAC)	business park
zone artisanale (ZA)	estate for small production companies
zone industrielle (ZI)	industrial estate

RENTING PREMISES

Most new businesses find renting more attractive. More funds are available for investment directly in the business and, in general, it is easier to move the business if larger premises are required later on. (More office space may well become available throughout France. Since June, 2005, residential property, including apartment blocks, in towns with populations of under 200,000 with the exception of those in the Ile de France 92, 93 and 94 *départe-*

ments no longer require special Prefectural authorisation to become business or professional premises.)

Whatever type of lease is signed, registration details of the business will be required which include the official address. So, unless your home address is going to be the registered office, temporary recourse to a *centre de domiciliation* (see pages 123–4) will be necessary. The landlord or their agent will also ask for proof of a comprehensive business risk assurance policy (*multi-risque professionnelle*) which should cover fire, theft, storm, snow, hail, electrical damage, burst pipes, civic responsibility related to the business' activity, natural disasters, etc.

Generally, leases contain a wider variety of possible clauses than property sales contracts. It is therefore advisable to get them checked by a qualified person/solicitor who understands exactly what they stipulate and also to ensure that any specially agreed clause to protect the tenant's interest is inserted.

Bail commercial

This is the classic business lease. It is established between '*le bailleur*' (the property owner) and the tenant, called '*le preneur*' or '*le locataire*'.

Tenants are strongly advised to pay particular care and attention to the following points which may or may not be expressed in contracts.

1. Any underestimation of the premises' features by the owner or his agent will not be grounds for a reduction in rent.

2. In the absence of an inventory and inspection of the premises and their fixtures and fittings, when the keys are handed over, the premises are deemed to be in perfect order.
    NB. The premises should always be inspected before occupation.

3. At least six months' notice by recorded delivery letter is required to terminate the nine-year lease at the end of each triennial period.

4. The tenant is entitled to continue to hold the lease after the initial nine years. A continuation lease should be signed for a further nine-year period to ensure that the annual rent review continues to be in line with, and not in excess of, the official *INSEE* building-cost/rent evaluation index which is updated every quarter.
    NB. Not all contracts include a clause confirming that the tenant has first refusal on a new lease.

5. If the tenant is an individual (*personne physique*) as opposed to a company they are entitled, subject to documentary proof, in the case of disability or retirement to cancel the lease contract at any time provided that at least six months' official notice is given.

6. Authorised business activities (*activités autorisées*) stipulated in the lease should cover, from the tenant's stand-point, all possible related activities which may be necessary to the development or evolution of the business. This is officially recognised as '*déspécialisation*'. (A point to consider also when the nature of the business is registered.)
    NB. Local exclusivity might be vital for some businesses and should be written into the lease if there are several other units available for rent to other businesses in the same property. The onus is also on the tenant to verify with local authorities that

their type of business will be officially authorised in the building and will not create a nuisance for other tenants; even if the lease is presented as a general-purpose lease '*bail tous commerces*' rather than a '*bail exclusif*' lease which details the type of business activity that can be undertaken.

7. The furniture and equipment supplied by the tenant should always equal the value of the rent and any other charges for which they are responsible.

   NB. Check that they are adequately insured against theft.

8. The tenant may be liable for replacement and repair of certain windows, including those that leak.

9. If basic changes to the structure or room lay-out of the premises are requested by the tenant, and authorised in writing by the owner, all costs including those of the building's architect will be borne by the tenant. At the end of the lease, any provisional and unauthorised modifications carried out by the tenant (for example partitions) must be completely removed.

10. The owner can carry out any work required to the building in general including any necessary plumbing within the premises rented without any compensation due to the tenant.

    NB. A question to ask before signing the lease is: are there any building plans envisaged which could affect the smooth running of the business?

11. Similarly, the tenant will not be entitled to any compensation in the event of any break-down in heating, telephone, water, electricity, gas services … including dustbin clearance.

    NB. The tenant pays maintenance charges and security charges on a pro-rata basis for the building either directly to the supplier or through the property owner and public utility services directly.

12. No compensation will be due to the tenant, from the owner, in the event of the building or premises being made subject to a compulsory purchase order.
13. The tenant, provided they have the approval of the property owner, can transfer the lease for the entire premises if they decide to sell their business. If a tenant is unable to find a buyer for their business they may offer the lease for a premium, the *droit au bail*, to a new tenant who must only use the premises for those business activities set out in the original lease.

A deposit (*dépôt de garantie*) representing three months' rent is usual. This is returnable, interest-free, at the end of the lease minus any repair costs outstanding. Letting agents' fees can be around 15 per cent of annual rent, a not inconsiderable percentage, especially if a *pas de porte* premium is asked for as well as the monthly rent.

Pas de porte is often expected for shops and other premises in prime sites and is calculated on what the owner foresees is the difference between the rent they could ask for in a free-market situation during the length of the *bail* and what they estimate will be the official increases permitted by the *INSEE* index. Although the tenant signs a nine-year lease with a classic *bail commercial*, if they think they may well use the triennial cancellation option an attempt to negotiate an appropriate reduction in the *pas de porte* would be logical.

The *bail professionnel* runs for a minimum six-year period and is designed for doctors, lawyers, chartered accountants/surveyors, etc. It is automatically extended if neither the tenant nor owner give six-months' officially recorded notice of cancellation. The owner is in a stronger position than with a *bail commercial* as they do not have to adhere to the *INSEE* rental index after six years or renew the lease with the out-going tenant.

Bail précaire (bail de courte durée)

This is the lease to use if the tenant is unsure of the future plans for their business, as it is a short-term lease running for a maximum of 23 months with a let-out (*résiliation*) option which can be exercised at any time provided two months official notice by recorded delivery letter is given. NB. The *résiliation* clause may not be included in the lease proposed, although you should ensure that it is.

Tenants who are still renting premises after 24 months are in fact normally entitled to sign a *bail commercial*, which is why the *bail précaire* is never more than 23 months, and, unlike the nine-year *bail commercial*, it is not renewable.

As with a *bail commercial*, special attention should be paid as to what type of businesses are generally permitted in the premises and to what particular business activity, allowing for *déspécialisation*, is written into the lease. A *bail précaire* which runs for more than 12 months is subject to the *INSEE* rental index so a *pas de porte* may be asked for.

The lease's general conditions should stipulate that premises will not be let out in the same building by the owner to a similar, competitive, business. In most other respects, the tenant of a *bail précaire* has the same responsibilities and liabilities as for a *bail commercial* and particularly with regard to points 7, 9 and 11 above. Transferring the lease is not, however, possible.

Letting agent's fees are normally expressed as a total amount, not as a percentage of annual rents as there will not be two annual amounts. Calculate what percentage the amount represents. While a *dépôt de garantie* will of course be necessary, the amount should be calculated according to the length of the lease. An amount representing three months' rent, for example, would be excessive.

Note that chambers of commerce or trade and town halls sometimes own premises suitable for artisans and small industries setting up, *ateliers relais*, which are available on *courte durée* leases at favourable rents. See also *Les pépiniéres d'entreprises.*

Crédit-bail

Leasing with an option to buy outright after several years for a price based on the premises' value at term less total rental amount paid is an interesting compromise. These kinds of rents are higher than for normal leases. However, property purchase is almost always a guaranteed investment. A *crédit-bail* lease should only be considered if the intention is to buy when the lease terminates.

USEFUL VOCABULARY

description des locaux	premises' inspection report
garantie des vices cachés	warranty of no hidden defects
location saisonnière	seasonal lease (for seasonal tourist businesses)
répartition des travaux	who-pays-what repairs lease clause
prestations	services
surface utile	usable office/workshop floor area including service areas

WORKING FROM HOME

This is an attractive and economic solution for many types of new businesses. It will undoubtedly appeal to a lot of foreigners who have moved to France to buy a better home and enjoy nicer surroundings. Although regulations make it increasingly easier to set up home-based businesses, strict discipline and organisation are necessary to ensure that family life will not intrude upon the working environment. Early risers can put in a few hours, getting paperwork up to date and planning for the day, before breakfast or incoming phone calls. Obviously, working/office hours should be set and adhered to, and the workplace should be clearly isolated from the rest of the home.

Home owners have four main possibilities:

◆ conversion of part of their existing residential accommodation (*surface habitable*) or non-habitable area such as the attic;
◆ conversion of an outside building on their plot;
◆ extending the house;
◆ or building special premises.

Old bourgeois houses, for example, with lofty ceilings and large windows are ideal for easy conversion to spacious through rooms – the French '*loft*' – suitable for artists studios, drawing offices or open-plan offices, perhaps with a mezzanine area. An attic conversion requires a ceiling height of at least 1.80 m and the floor and property foundations must be checked to ensure that they are adequate to support continual use. All conversion projects to an area of over 170 m², and extension projects of over 20 m² floor area producing a total new floor area of over 170 m², must be accompanied by an architect's plans when application for planning permission is made. Note that planning permission is necessary for any conversion that changes the use of a building or part of a building, so even a conversion of a single garage – one-car garages average 15 m^2 – requires application for a *permis de construire*.

Any new building plan proposing more than 20 m^2 floor area requires planning permission which will of course be subject to any remaining planning permission density for the plot. New garden sheds of any description, provided they're over 20 m^2, are included.

A *permis de construire* is valid for two years: enough time to change your mind if the whole project needs rethinking. It can also be extended if you give notice two months before the initial two-year deadline is reached. Work has to have been physically started within the valid period and announced by an outside notice-board – all extra publicity – giving the property owner's name, size of new floor areas, any new roof heights and stating what work is being carried out.

One third of your household's utility bills are taken by tax authorities as tax-deductible business expenses, unless an extension or conversion for the business can be shown to occupy more than one third of the overall floor space. Don't forget, if you are installing a separate business phone line, to get the preferential *professionnel* rental rate from France Télécom and to compare the cost of their phone calls and Internet connection packages which correspond to your call and connection needs against those offered by other operators such as Cégétél and Télé2.

A property owner's main residence and a property rented by tenants as their main residence can be used as their business premises provided they do not receive customers or use the property to receive and warehouse goods. Landlords of rented properties should be notified in writing by recorded delivery of this intention. Even if the lease is exclusively residential (*bail à usage exclusif d'habitation*) it can be used for business provided this is notified.

By contrast a *bail mixte* – for professional and residential use – which runs for three years like a residential lease if the tenant is an individual (*personne physique*), and six years for companies, does not require the property to be the main residence. Non-trading professions such as doctors and lawyers use it to locate their practices in residential buildings.

The August 2003 *Loi Dutreuil* economic initiative law simplified new business regulations and conditions. *SARL* limited companies can now use the home address of their managing director, in rented or owned property, as their head office address. Even if the residential lease or private estate regulations normally forbid this, a maximum period of five years is now allowed. This will give sufficient time for most new companies establishing themselves.

BUSINESS CENTRES (*CENTRES D'AFFAIRES*)
These offer a wide range of office services, all of which can be used quite independently of each other, including *domiciliation* address, furnished and heated offices on short-term leases, secretarial and photocopying services, and rooms for meetings. They can also provide information and contacts to assist with legal and financial

formalities when setting up the business, undertake mailing operations to selected addresses as part of an initial marketing plan, and offer translation services.

Businesses that need to test their market before investing in office equipment, secretaries and longer term commitments to premises have the possibility of using modern well-equipped offices in prime localities and often with private parking spaces. Also, those whose funds are slender in the initial months of the business will not have to have office furnishings, fittings and equipment to equal at least the value of monthly rent as stipulated in standard business premises' leases. They are also the solution for small companies that just need a first-class address for their registered office. A business centre that is a member of the national federation, *Syndicat national des centres d'affaires et de domiciliation* (*SNCAED*), 22, rue de la Pépinière, 75008 Paris (www.sncaed.com) is recommended as the *SNCAED* publish a guide setting out minimum service standards required from their members.

Here is an example of basic services that can be provided, and points that should be checked, with an indication of monthly prices exclusive of VAT (*HT*) :

- *Domiciliation* (having the address): up to 90€.
- *Permanence téléphonique* (switchboard service). Sliding-scale linked to number of calls bands: from approximately 60€.
- Direct line: approximately 30€.
- Plus the cost of outgoing calls made. How promptly can the switchboard reply? Is there an English-speaking person to handle calls from English-speaking customers? Are the offices

open throughout the day without any lunchtime closing and possibly on Saturday mornings?

- *Routage* (mailing on letters): up to 20 per cent on the re-postage stamp cost.
- Is mail reposted the same day, and in adequate envelopes?

Bureaux équipés (fitted and furnished offices)

- Prices vary for renting a furnished, heated office for three months to 12 months (with quarterly option to cancel), but around 600€ a month would not be unreasonable. Look for around 15 m² for one person who receives visitors. Computers will not usually be supplied. Expect to be asked for a *dépôt de garantie* for up to three months' rent.

Secrétariat

- Hourly labour rate: approximately 30€.
- Extremely useful for producing reports and business letters in correct French from notes and dictation.
- Letters (per page in black type): approximately 5€.
- Tabular presentation (per page in black type): 9 to 15€.
- Colour tabular presentations and English text typing cost more. Urgent jobs, which have not been pre-booked will also cost more.
- Photocopying costs about 0.10€ a copy which is about the same price as in a Post Office where quality can be inferior.
- Internet with permanent broadband (*ADSL*) access: approximately 25€.
- *Salle de réunion* (meeting rooms) seating 20 people: per day, approximately 80€ and per half-day, approximately 55€.

A good business centre should have a choice of different-sized meeting rooms, with one available for last-minute bookings. Audio-visual equipment, at additional cost, should also be available on request.

Smaller office rooms suitable for receiving customers or clients for individual interviews or meetings should also be available on an hourly or daily basis, at a correspondingly reduced price.

Most *centres d'affaires* will have a small refectory area with vending machines which can be ideal for getting to know the other tenants.

LES PEPINIERES D'ENTREPRISES

These premises have a vocational *raison d'être* rather than a business one as they are run or have been created by professional federations or local authorities for the sole purpose of helping new businesses to develop.

While they offer services comparable to those of *centres d'affaires*, premises are rented for up to 24 months at extremely favourable prices, and usually with the possibility of a further 12-month period, taking new businesses through the critical first three years. Assistance and advice is given throughout this period. It is claimed that businesses which emerge from *pépinières* have a much greater chance of long-term success than others.

ZFU, ZRU AND *ZUS* DEVELOPMENT AREAS

While these areas can offer new businesses attractive tax or social security contribution exemptions, they should not necessarily be considered as good sites. They are by definition in depressed areas, which will not help businesses that require an established booming local economy to help them grow. Furthermore, the criteria demanded to obtain these advantages varies, with the emphasis on the creation of new salaried employment, so qualification is by no means automatic for small businesses. (The exemptions can be granted to new businesses, *and* established businesses employing up to 50 people, such as factories moving into the area.) Small-business activities that do not require a prestigious *lieu d'exercice d'activité*, or a healthy local market, for example those relying on correspondence and Internet orders and who take on staff have nothing to lose by applying. A better address for *domiciliation*, in this instance for incoming post, can always be set up in a *centre d'affaires*.

Zones franches urbaines (ZFU)

Visit the website www.wille.gouv.fr to see where they are based. Most are in the Northern part of France. Tax exemption for five years on profits, *taxe professionnelle* (local business tax) and *taxe foncière* (land tax) can apply, as can employers' exemptions for five years, to social security contributions based on up to 1.5 times the national minimum salary if there is at least one full-time employee.

Zones de redynamisation urbaine (ZRU) and Zones urbaines sensibles (ZUS)

A ZRU is an urban area with a particularly high unemployment rate – the national unemployment rate is around 10 per cent – and a *ZUS* is an urban area with old neglected houses. *ZRUs*, of which there are now over 400, will no doubt replace the *ZFU* system. There are over 700 *ZUS* areas throughout France. For a list of

ZUS locations enter 'zus' in the search panel of your Internet search engine and click on the website www.i.ville.gouv.fr/divbib/doc/ chercherZUS.htm.

In both development categories employers' contributions to social security contributions, based on up to 1.5 times the minimum salary, are exempt for 12 months provided there is at least one full-time employee.

BUSINESS LOCATION CHECKLIST

France is a vast country with three coasts, mountainous areas and great tracts of sparsely populated countryside. If residence and a business are being set up at the same time don't overlook the following.

◆ Is the location well placed for easy access to major economic areas and towns?

◆ Are motorways within easy reach, and airports/cargo seaports if export is going to be part of the business?

◆ With future expansion and taking on staff in mind, is there a good pool of qualified staff available from local universities and training centres? Students in France tend to come from the areas in which they were brought up so they will also have first-hand local knowledge.

◆ Is the area one with a lot of new businesses starting up and specialist advice available?

◆ Is the area near one of the new poles of competitiveness and excellence (for research and development companies) approved and financially aided by the government? These areas promise a dynamic economic future. They are spread throughout France. Visit www.competitivite.gouv.fr for precise locations. Interestingly, the Limousin *région* which is increasingly popular with British buyers of residential property, on account, perhaps, of its mainly rural landscape, only has one.

◆ Is there a good supply of immediately available premises and business parks?

◆ Are hospitals and clinics, GPs and specialists, child-care centres and schools for the family available? What about old people's homes for later on in life?

◆ What about the natural scenery, beaches, leisure and sporting facilities when you have time off?

◆ Is there a wide range of historical and cultural sites, cinemas and theatres? Plus any other activities for culture vultures?

You should try to visit areas several times before deciding where to set up home and business. If you decide to move home again later on remember that legal and estate agency fees are about twice those in the UK.

USEFUL VOCABULARY

atelier	studio or workshop
cloison	partition
courriel	email
salle de formation	training room
taux de chômage	unemployment rate
traitement de texte	word processing

OFFICE LAYOUT, FITTINGS AND EQUIPMENT

Completely open-plan, half-partitioned or private offices are the available options with rented or purchased premises. If customers visit, a reception counter with easy chairs will be needed in addition to comfortable and practical office furniture. Sun-blinds may be necessary later on if you move premises in the winter to a normally sunny area, where the previous tenant has removed the blinds that they fitted.

Trade cash-and-carry office equipment suppliers such as Métro have inexpensive quality goods. Obtain a customer card once you have received the registration certificate (*k bis extrait*) for the business from the *centre des formalités des entreprises*. Stationery supplies can be easily ordered at keen prices from the catalogues of mail-order suppliers, such as Viking, with a fast turn-around service.

Review the possibilities of your existing computer. Do you have a basic word-processing program for correspondence and creation of customer files? Is a simple accounts program (*logiciel compt-abilité*) compatible? What other programs will you need and will they be compatible? Have you made the most of possible telephone and computer link-ups? Can an incoming customer call automatically open up their file on your computer screen?

Don't forget to check the alarm system or have one installed, whether you rent or buy premises, and check any property regulations limiting what can be installed. Modern *télésurveillance* alarm systems use pre-selected, confidential radio wave frequencies linked to a central monitoring office assuring around-the-clock surveillance. The service and costs of hiring and installing intrusion detectors are included in the rental contract. It is best to install a package which includes heat-sensitive or movement-scanning detectors *and* alarm sirens and strobe lights (*avertisseurs*), as there is always an initial delay, while you or someone who has agreed, in your absence, to accept calls are phoned to see if the signal received is not a false alarm.

BROADBAND CONNECTION

There are about 11 million broadband subscribers in France, just about the same number as in the UK. Most urban areas are equipped with telephone exchange systems which can cope with broadband (known as *ADSL* or *haut débit*) speeds and the government and local authorities have a firm intention to complete broadband connection possibility throughout France by the end of 2007. However, some isolated, rural areas will no doubt still be unable to connect to broadband after this date. This is an essential point to consider if the plan is to establish an Internet-based business in a remote area.

The overall business and private Internet market in France is shared principally amongst the following providers (*fournisseurs d'access Internet (FAI)*): Alice/Tiscali (part of Télécom Italia), Cégétel, Club-Internet, Free, Neuf Télécom, AOL, Télé 2, and Wanadoo with France Télécom. Broadband contracts usually propose rental of the special modem required for approximately 3 or 4 euros a month, and generally run for a minimum of one year, with an obligatory renewal reminder at least one month before the renewal date. If there is no minimum contract period there will be a contract cancellation charge.

Prices and special introductory offers for an initial period are continuously changing and follow increasing demand in an increasingly competitive market. The www.comparatifadsl.net

website provides regularly updated comparison tables of prices and features offered by Internet providers. Just click on the Internet provider shown in the table to access their website for fuller details of their various broadband packages. The Consumers' Association magazine *Que Choisir* also provides periodic reports on the comparative reliability of *FAI*s through their website: www.quechoisir.fr.

Read rental contracts carefully before making a choice. Some particular points to note and questions to have in mind are:

* Will it be more advantageous or not to use a provider offering unlimited free phone calls (usually to numbers within France only) through a *dégroupage* telephone network? While France Télécom offer preferential call rates for businesses and also for pre-selected phone numbers, *dégroupage* connection bypasses France Télécom exchanges meaning that renting a telephone line with France Télécom is no longer necessary.
* Initial offers at greatly reduced monthly rental amounts are usually followed by a substantial monthly increase with the new rental amount.
* What do calls cost to the special assistance lines if there is a problem with the Internet connection? These calls will not be part of any unlimited free calls package. What is the average waiting time before you are actually put through to someone? There is increasing governmental pressure on providers to make this 'waiting time' free of charge, but at the moment it's still charged. Some providers that *do* have a no-charge assistance line are notoriously difficult to get through to.

- Can a rental agreement be signed up by post using a direct debit bank form rather than by completing credit/debit card details online?

  In the event of cancellation, experience is that rental agreements which were concluded on-line are often not cancelled immediately.

  While it may be possible to phone and cancel a contract (before its renewal date), phoning to cancel is not recommended. Always send a recorded delivery letter (*lettre recommandée avec accusé de réception*) and keep a copy on file. Even with annual contracts there may be a cancellation charge.

- All providers should indicate in which areas they offer *ADSL* and if a *dégroupée* network can be used.

8

Procedures

The administrative process for registration has been greatly simplified by the 2003 Dutreuil law.

Before registration procedures have been completed certain commitments will no doubt already have been made and taken on behalf of the new *EI* or company being set up. Knowing what can and should be done before signing the articles, *in the case of companies*, and then before the official registration certificate is received is particularly important. Make a list of what has been done and/or promised and keep it with the proposed articles before they are signed. The company as a legal identity (*personne morale*) will then take over liability for these acts and commitments which up to that moment have been the personal responsibility of its future partners.

When the articles have been signed the principal entrepreneur should be officially mandated by the partners to sign contracts on behalf of the company for business premises, purchases, staff, etc. Ideally, the business should start trading after all these initial contracts have been signed.

If applying for a patent (see Chapter 1) await its acceptance before publicising the project or product. Acceptance normally takes about three weeks. No reply within five months means that the patent application has been accepted.

The bank account for the business is established as soon as any required capital is paid up, but cannot be used until registration has been completed.

Registration formalities

The *CFE*s (*centres de formalités des entreprises*) are the registration organisations for all the necessary formalities when starting a business. One file is deposited in one office containing all the required paperwork. Ensure the forms requesting information are filled in correctly and all the documents required are supplied at the same time, otherwise the whole registration process will be delayed. Each *CFE* covers a geographical area. There are different *CFE*s for different types of business activities and different types of business structure.

The table overleaf is a guide to the main *CFE*s and their applications.

Any subsequent changes to the business (a move elsewhere, change in name, change in business structure, change in type of business, change in partners, capital, directors, and marital status for *EI*s, etc.) must be notified to the *CFE* where the business was originally registered.

Initial registration, since February 2005, can now be effected online via the Internet. The registration receipt (*Récépissé de dépôt de création d'entreprise* (*RDCE*) now has legal value and states that a registration number for the new business is awaited. It is accepted immediately by banks providing loans, and by France Télécom providing phone lines at business rates, as proof of the business' future existence.

Table 8.1 *CFEs* and their applications

Commerçants, *Sociétés commerciales* *(SARL, SA, SCOP, EURL, SNC)*	Chambre de commerce et d'industrie
Artisans listed on the trades register (*Répertoires des métiers*), Individuals (*personnes physiques*), *Sociétés*	Chambre de métiers
Sociétés civiles (*SCI, SCM, SCP*), *Sociétés d'exercice libéral* (*SELARL, SELCA, SELU*), Non-salaried sales agents (*EI*s)	Greffe du tribunal de commerce
All professional/service (*EI*) businesses	URSSAF
Writers and artists who invoice VAT and who either pay *IR* (*BIC*) tax or *IS* tax, and are not in the above categories	Centre des impôts
Individual farmers and farming companies	Chambre d'agriculture

All businesses subsequently receive a 14-digit identification *SIRET* number which is composed of the legal identity *SIREN* number – the first nine digits – and the internal classification number (*NIC*) – the last five digits. This number pinpoints where the business is located. The business code (*NAF*) classification number is also received at the same time and the actual business registration certificate, known as '*extrait K*' for *EI*s and '*extraits K bis*' for companies, later on.

It may be possible to start the business activity while awaiting the *SIRET*. It is recommended that this is checked as soon as the *RDCE* is issued.

Strictly speaking there is no registration fee, but in practice most *CFE*s charge an administrative fee, from around 30€ in a Tribunal de Commerce for an *EI* up to around 300€ for a *SA* or *SAS* company. There is no registration fee with URSSAF.

As soon as the business is officially registered this must be announced in the local press and in the national civil- and commercial-announcements journal, *BODDAC*. Local newspapers may accept deferred payment. Essential information is the type of legal structure, name of the business, capital amount (if applicable), registered address, business activity, period of existence and the full name and address of the manager or entrepreneur running the business, and the registration office. The date the business is set up is often included. If not the date of the announcement suffices. Below is a typical announcement for an *EURL*:

Avis de constitution

Avis est donné de la constitution d'une société présentant les caractéristiques suivantes:

Forme: EURL

Dénomination: France

...

Capital: 1.000€

Siège social: 99, boulevard .... 75001 Paris

Objet: ....

Durée: 99 ans

Gérance: Monsieur Claude DUPONT, 6 chemin ... 75001 Paris

Immatriculation (registration)*: RCS de Paris (1ère arrondissement)*

All businesses should check they have done the following:

- opened a bank account;
- advised La Poste of where they are;
- made themselves known or become a member of their trade/professional federation;
- registered within three months with an *ARRCO* complementary pensions office even if there are no salaried staff immediately;
- taken out business and personal insurance policies. (Obtain information from the *CDIA* (*centre de documentation et d'information de l'assurance*) Visit www.cdia.fr.

Companies should also:

- register their articles with their tax office;
- deposit cash capital in a frozen account, and have any capital provided in kind officially evaluated by a *commissaire aux apports*.

(9)

Avoiding pitfalls

Certain stumbling blocks or unnecessary expenses can be avoided at the start of the business.

Improve your French

While imperfection in speech can be used, initially, as a commercial ploy it is essential to understand 100 per cent of what is being said and written. Even if you never, attain absolute fluency in your written or language skills, it is important that you can understand what other people write and speak. Writing out cheques correctly is also essential. The first and second lines on cheques are for the amount in words while the following line, commencing '*A*' is for the payee's name: not the other way round. For numbers, written (and printed/typed) decimal points become commas, the number 7 should be written with a horizontal line through the stem and dots should be inserted between thousands. For example, a British £5,000.52 becomes £5.000,52.

The project

Don't rush into something completely new to you just because France is a foreign country. Illogically, you may feel prepared to do things you would not even think of attempting in the UK.

If you do decide to change direction completely be prepared to invest time in a training course.

Setting up the business

Define the idea; check out its feasibility through market research; get the business plan checked over by an accountant; decide on the legal form verifying with a specialist that it suits the project and its potential; ascertain the necessity for any outside finance, grants and/or loans and obtain them; the legal form decided, find the premises and complete registration of the business, with creation of the business' bank account and capital deposited for limited companies.

Employees

If you do decide to have employees, check that European Union (EU) citizens have a residence permit (*carte de séjour*) and that other nationalities have the right to live and work in France. Penalties are severe for EU employers – who must of course have their own *carte de séjour* – employing people who are not entitled to work in France. Note that while *EI*s can employ salaried staff it may be more convenient to sub-contract work (make sure the outside contractor is registered).

Estimates

Don't miss out essential costs and destroy your profit. Detailed estimates are a legal requirement and help you explain/justify prices. Clear, reasonably priced estimates will obtain orders.

Getting advice

Free specialist trade advice can be obtained from the Chambre de l'Agriculture for farmers and wine-growers, the Chambre des Métiers for artisans and the Chambre de Commerce et Industrie and also from national federations or organisations which cover these and all other categories. Being independent is, in a reasonable measure, an appropriate quality for entrepreneurs, but *don't* try to unravel accounting and legal formalities without professional advice.

Drawing up most legal papers and contracts (*actes*) by notaries are subject to set national fees (*émoluments*). A *notaire* should therefore inform you beforehand (ask if the information is not forthcoming) of the fee for any particular *acte*. It is even more important to know beforehand the *notaires* fee for any contract or preparation of any official document which is not subject to a set rate. *Notaire honoraires* for their advice or consultation on matters such as family and property settlements are *not* subject to set fees. Ask for a costing beforehand implying that instruction for an *acte* will follow a reasonable *honoraire*. There are around 8,000 notaries in France for approximately 35,000 communities. It is usual, however, to use a property owner's *notaire* when buying a property, but it is not obligatory.

Fees for consulting a solicitor (*avocat*) may vary from practice to practice even though they may not be negotiable. The price given should include VAT, except if it is a small solicitor's practice classed as a *micro-entreprise*. You may even be asked to pay cash for a consultation – you will be provided with an invoice of course – but you don't have to accept this request. Consult the *Yellow Pages* or www.pagesjaunes.fr under *avocats spécialistes* for business solicitors. If possible obtain a recommendation for a solicitor from someone who understands exactly what you want to do.

Get advice from an accountant on how to do the accounts, and, ideally, one who has worked in a tax office, even if the type of business means that you can do the necessary book-keeping yourself. Like using an architect to redesign a property, it will usually save you at least what it costs you.

Don't let cheques bounce. If a cheque is not honoured within 30 days, no further cheques can be written through any bank in France for five years. The business will be seriously hampered.

Don't postdate cheques as it's illegal.

Getting things confirmed

Get any prices, delivery periods, etc. confirmed in writing. A little Anglo-Saxon insistence on this may be necessary. As you're not French, this can be your excuse.

Getting experience

If you have the opportunity, get some experience of what you propose to do by working beforehand for someone, even if it's only for a short time. This is particularly useful if your business project is a complete change to what you've always done previously. Check that employment contract exclusion clauses *do not* prevent you doing this.

Getting loans

Lay all your cards on the table when asking for loans and show proof of what other loans have been obtained or are promised. Loans are often dependent on others being obtained.

Getting an overdraft

Don't apply to your bank for overdraft facilities (*droit de découvert*) at the last moment. Anticipate this contingency well beforehand and ask when your bank balance is healthy.

Insurance

Double-check with someone who is familiar with your business that the *multi-risque* policy you're planning to take out does provide all the necessary personal, business and third-party cover.

Marketing and market research

Beware of getting on the band wagon of *tendance* (passing fashion) products which can die a sudden death. Be prepared to adapt the business, introduce a new, but associated activity or product, sell to a new sector in the market, or have another separate business running alongside if the original plan doesn't find a sufficiently large market. You should test-market, if possible, before committing yourself.

Negotiating

Drive hard bargains for prices and payment terms with suppliers, but *don't* be impossible and *don't* renege on what has been agreed. The French are used to driving hard bargains.

Objectives

Objectives should be realistically attainable and not idealistic. On a daily basis allow time for seeking out new business, hiving off administrative and accounting work as much as possible, but not forgetting to make sure it's done properly.

Opening hours for shops

Keep to the general opening and closing at midday hours if you are a shop in a high-street shopping area, particularly if you want to keep up with competitors who may belong to the same trade federation. High-street hairdressers are nearly always closed on

Mondays. Perhaps take premises in a *centre commercial* if you want to remain open throughout the whole day.

However, estate agents are an exception. If you are qualified to start an *agence immobilière* consider advertising weekend house visiting and office opening hours. It will give you a competitive edge. A lot of estate agents don't work over the weekends and be prepared to stick to weekend working if you start off with it. You should also remain open on weekdays.

Partners
While partnerships provide necessary complementary skills for entrepreneurs who would not be able to start and run their businesses by themselves, it is estimated that up to 15 per cent of businesses fail because partners fall out or cannot effectively work together. Having a partner will certainly help rather than hinder applications for finance from banks and other private sources. An ideal partner in France would be one with hands-on French accountancy knowledge and good administrative experience leaving the entrepreneur time to create new products and ideas, market the business and develop new and existing customers.

Not being able to agree on major decisions concerning the company's direction or progress is one thing but actually being able to work together on a daily basis is another. Although over 800,000 businesses in France are husband and wife teams, a couple moving to France who have previously worked independently in separate jobs may find that running a bed and breakfast business together does not work out.

To protect a spouse's interest in the event that a family business may have to be wound up it is advisable to make them a salaried employee (see Chapter 11 for details).

Don't take on a partner purely because of the financial assistance they will bring to the company, and avoid 50/50 capital shares which may lead to no go situations.

Premises

Rental amounts for premises or *pas de porte* amounts linked to leases may be negotiable. Property for sale prices should always be treated as possibly negotiable.

Finding suitably situated premises may take time if location is all important, especially if you are not living in France before staring the business. You should allow enough time to search for suitable premises.

Procedures

Tick off all items as they are completed in the Procedures chapter. If you are not yet living in France, things will usually take longer than if you were in the country. Any registration paperwork must be immaculate. You should ensure that you allow for the time factor in your plans.

Purchasing equipment

Don't be penny-wise with essential equipment and business vehicles – always pay for quality. Breakdowns are not recommended when reliability and respecting delivery deadlines are vital, especially at the start of the business. Smoothly transacted business will produce welcome cash, lead to more from the same source and recommendations to other potential customers.

Registration

Ensure that you have obtained your business registration number or certified proof that it's on the way. Without it you won't be able to open a business trading account and obtain a business cheque book.

Regulations

There are strict regulations governing environment protection, hygiene, pricing products and services, descriptions on packaging and the packaging material itself, what you can and cannot say in publicity messages, international trade requirements, different licences for selling alcohol (with or without accompanying food), etc. Office premises being converted to a restaurant, for example, will need to meet several new requirements. Make sure the business is *en règle* (conforms to requirements) and check if any new regulations are in the offing which should be taken into account. There is no point in having stock impounded or withdrawn from the market just when you are starting out. The following authorities will confirm regulations in force:

DDASS: direction départementale des affaires sanitaires et sociales (hygiene in areas frequented by the public).

SDIS: service départementale d'incendie et de secours (fire and safety).

DSV: direction départementale des services vétérinaries (food and animal hygiene).

DDCRF: direction départementale de la concurrence de la consommation et de la répression des fraudes (product descriptions, labelling and various other regulations).

Selling
Don't retail anything below cost price unless you have obtained prefectoral permission, or unless it is during the official winter and summer *'Soldes'* (Sales) periods.

Specialisation
This usually pays, but *don't* create something too far ahead of its time or too Anglo-Saxon for French tastes, that nobody understands or will take a long time to understand before they want to buy it.

Teething problems
Inevitably there will be teething problems. Follow the business plan, without panicking, remembering that it has been thoroughly checked and created with an accountant, anticipating at the same time the possible need for modifications, to develop new strategies and obtain extra finance if there is a major increase in product demand or market changes.

Keep tabs on the cash-flow position, and *don't* confuse healthy cash-flow with healthy profits. Cut costs immediately if there are cash-flow problems. If the problems are serious don't hesitate to dismiss staff, respecting the correct procedure (see Chapter 11) before they affect the very survival of the business.

The weather

Anticipate a possible changing-weather factor if agricultural produce, plantations, orchards, etc., are entirely dependent upon a stable, predictable climate. The weather is becoming increasingly unpredictable, particularly in the South-Western parts of France with either too much rain or not enough.

PART 2

Running the business

(10)

The accounts and correspondence

CENTRES DE GESTIONS AGRÉÉS (CGA)

These officially approved (*agréé*) non-profit making organisations will check annually, using professional accountants, that accounts balance (*rapprochement de comptes*) and are correctly kept by their small-business members, and will undertake to present their income tax returns to the tax authorities. They will check that business expenses are claimed correctly against tax. For example, the cost of vehicle insurance *cannot* be added to the kilometre allowance covering cost of running and depreciation of a business vehicle. They also supply special day books with separate columns for different types of costs and expenses. Social security contributions, for example, can be easily distinguished from office stationery purchases.

Members must be registered either with a chamber of commerce and industry or a *chambre des métiers*. A *CGA* can also offer their advice on positive and negative points in the annual returns and provide market information on a regular basis relating to the business' particular field. Both *CGA*s and *AGA*s (see page 153) also try to foresee and solve financial problems which would otherwise lead to business failures (*liquidations judiciaires*) or appointment of a receiver to draw up a recovery plan (*redressements judiciaires*).

But don't expect them to produce debtors to sales, stock to sales, and stock to purchases ratios for management purposes. Since January 2006 the new *sauvegarde des entreprises* law enables *commercants* and *artisans* who foresee difficulty with their business to negotiate, with the aid of an officially appointed councilator (*conciliateur*), extended credit with their suppliers. However, if a business has already been unable to meet its commitments for more than 45 days it must go into liquidation (*déposer le bilan*).

It is worth noting that, statistically, members of the *CGA* are much less likely to have an inspection of their accounts (*contrôle fiscale*) (which can last some months) by their tax office.

Members are also entitled to certain tax allowances including deduction of spouse's salary in family businesses, provided the business is registered for VAT (*TVA*) and pays income tax under the personal income declaration classification (*impôt sur le revenue*). Membership fees, which include the cost of the professional accountants' service, are tax deductible. The Finance Law for 2006 proposes some new measures for *CGA*s and *AGA*s which will apply, in 2007, on income produced in 2006. Full details can be found on the www.apce.com website under '*loi de finance pour 2006*'. Why not make an appointment to see your tax inspector and see whether the latest regulations will be to your advantage?

To qualify, application for membership is required within three months of starting a business or within three months of the start of a business' new financial year.

Businesses can display their membership details on their letter headed paper, indicating to both suppliers and potential customers that the new business they are dealing with is a reliable business going about their administrative affairs in a sensible manner. *CGA* membership also means that payments by cheque made out to the business will always be accepted. This must be announced in literature or displayed prominently on the premises. Cash payments are, of course, still accepted, but 'cash only' signs are out. It is reassuring to know that it is a serious matter to issue a cheque that bounces. Unused cheques and any bank credit cards must be returned by the guilty party to their bank if payment is not honoured and a fine of 15 per cent if not paid within 30 days. Otherwise a five-year ban on writing cheques delivered by any French bank is enforced by the central Banque de France.

Most companies (*sociétés*), other than *EURL*s and family *SARL*s, pay tax under the *impôt sur sociétés* declaration classification. They can however still join a *CGA*, although they will not be entitled to any tax relief or allowances as members.

Les associations de gestions agréés: (AGA)
Similar to a *CGA*, an *AGA* provides financial advice and assistance from a professional accountant. Around 80 different self-employed professional activities covering insurance, business-to-business, computer, cultural, financial, health assurance, social and training services come under the *AGA* umbrella. Membership, as with *CGA* membership, brings certain tax advantages.

For a list of *CGA*s, contact the Fédération des centres de gestion agréés, 2 rue Meissonnier, 75017 Paris or visit www.fcga.fr.

For a list of *AGA*s, write to Union nationale des associations agréées, 36 rue de Picpus, 75012 Paris or visit www.unasa.org.

To locate a *CGA* or *AGA* locally consult the *Yellow Pages* under *centres et associations de gestion agréés* or visit www.pagesjaunes.fr.

ACCOUNTING PRINCIPLES

Although a *CGA* or *AGA* will ensure that annual returns are prepared and presented correctly to the tax authorities, they will not be behind you or the person who does your bookkeeping entries (*écritures*) every day. It is vital, especially for entrepreneurs with no accounting experience at all, to have a basic grasp of accounting and also to understand the requirements of the French system. A one-man artisan entrepreneur, planning ahead, doing the selling, producing the goods and negotiating the purchase and payment terms for supplies needs to understand exactly what financial impact his actions and decisions will have upon his business.

Keeping the accounts up to date is the best way to avoid potential business problems before they become irremediable, eliminate errors, prevent fraud and generally protect and manage the business' assets. Look ahead … healthy accounts will encourage banks, new suppliers and important new customers which need to be supplied regularly to work with developing businesses. (Key suppliers and customers can go out of business overnight and replacements will be required immediately.)

The need to note and file papers in an orderly fashion covering deliveries, payments due and payments made is at the heart of all accounting. Estimates (*devis*) issued for new business, even if they come to nothing, should be filed for two years. Note that deposits received from customers are either *arrhes* which are refunded to twice their value if the business fails to supply or firm-commitment *acomptes* with balance of the order amount due from the customer if they cancel. If you are certain that your business can supply specially-produced or non-stock goods or have available the rental holiday accommodation etc. within or at the time agreed, only accept an *acompte*. *La comptabilité générale* records all business transactions. The assets (*actif*) and liabilities (*passif*) and any resulting profit must be shown in a statement of accounts (*bilan*) covering not more than a 12-month period – the financial year – and within three months of the end of that period.

Entreprises individuelles need to record their expenses and receipts on a daily basis and a *CGA/AGA* will explain exactly how this should be done. All limited companies, who must keep all invoices and receipts for expenses, also have to maintain an assets and liabilities book (*livre inventaire*); a day book (*livre journal*); annual returns ledger (*grand livre*); a pay book (*livre de paie*); staff register (*registre du personnel*) and, of course, a minutes book (*livre d'assemblée*). These special books are supplied by office stationers, and their pages must be initialled and officially numbered by the clerk to the commercial court (*greffe du tribunal de commerce*). All entries (*écritures*) must be immaculately written or typed without any alterations.

Livres journal and *livres inventaire, as well as business correspondence*, must be kept for 10 years and staff salary slips, registers and social security payment details for five years. Correctly maintained accounts certified by an accountant are acceptable exhibits in litigation cases. The association of chartered accountants' website is www.experts-comptables.fr.

CORRESPONDENCE

While email messages to other businesses can be relatively informal, such as memos between internal departments, letters to other businesses, customers and government departments must follow the traditional forms of opening and conclusion. You don't have to have a *diplôme* in French business administration, but it is advisable to use a secretarial service (see *Centre d'affaires* in Chapter 7) to prepare certain standard letters which can be easily adapted or consider employing a bilingual secretary, who can, for example, also do the accounts, to ensure that the content (*le fond*) as well as the style (*la forme*) are correct. Translation by a certified translator (*traducteur assermenté*) of documents such as birth, death, marriage and divorce certificates may be necessary for official business purposes and the British Embassy or Consulate office have lists of these translators. The translation fees are laid down and are not negotiable.

Although you may not be actually typing business letters you should know some basic rules for layout.

The addressee should be in the top right-hand corner of the page and preceded by the town (from where the letter is written) and the date, e.g.:

Paris, le 1er aôut, 2006

Monsieur Pierre DUPONT
Responsable d'achats
SARL Bruno
107, route de Paris
69000 Lyon

Note that the months never have capital letters and only the 1st of the month is written '1er'. Otherwise dates are written as 'le 2', 'le 3', etc. The French Post Office ask for no commas to be inserted between address lines on envelopes to speed up the sorting process. It is standard practice with all letters to write the name and address of the sender on the reverse or top left-hand corner of the envelope to ensure that any 'gone-away' mail can be returned, unopened, to the sender.

USEFUL VOCABULARY

agré(é)	authorised
bulletin de paie	salary slip
cheque 'en bois'	a cheque that 'bounces'
écritures	book-keeping entries

Getting and keeping customers

MARKETING

The right product or service for the right niche is one thing. Launching it, getting it known and modifying it to keep abreast of trends (*tendances*) in the French market is another. Almost instant acceptance is required by potential customers so that a small business is up and running from day one. The French consumer is particularly demanding and expects nothing less than first-class service as a standard part of the product (or service). Originality or something trend-setting, but with a long-term future, which goes further than standard practice should be the aim.

A short-term marketing plan for the most effective promotion of the business and what it offers, to obtain customers from the existing market sector, should be built into the initial three-year forecast. As a guide, cost this at around 5 per cent of projected turnover. The number of transactions and contracts to be completed or products to be sold and their prices must also be established. A medium-term plan which will come into operation after the first three to five years should consider how the organisation – perhaps the legal form – of the business should be modified and possibly the product ranges and the way they are sold.

Most of what the business offers will be the result of the previous market research confirming that original ideas were the right ones or adapting them, if necessary, to the requirements of the targeted market. Garden furniture, for example, promoted directly to high-rise flat occupants will not be of interest to these occupants if they have no means of using it. Furniture suitable for small balconies would be more suitable.

Who actually pays and who influences the buying decision for products should be known. Indeed, it may be a joint decision. Mums pay for what children want, and children are very persuasive in France. Pocket money is not as customary as in the UK and young children are forbidden by law to do occasional work to earn themselves money. Shopping for food is often delegated to husbands who take more interest in this than husbands in the UK and will consult their wives by mobile phone to check a product or suggest an additional purchase. The over 50s (*troisième age*) age group should not be neglected. They now represent (with the over 75s (*quatrième age*)) up to 50 per cent of disposable income in France. Home-help services for the over 75s is a big growth area. People are living longer and many born in the post-war baby boom are now coming up for retirement with plenty of (shopping) time and sizeable pensions. Attracting and keeping the same customers (*fidélisation*) through several decades is a new concept to be remembered with product development.

Despite the growth of discount food supermarkets, the French market is still very attracted to sales promotions and special offers which emphasise extra product rather than having to pay less. The authorised summer and winter sales which *are* about price are something else. The price reduction periods are strictly controlled and the reduced price or the percentage reduction and the original price must be clearly shown. Luxury branded products such as perfumes remain a classic exception. Reputation will not be jeopardised for de luxe products by special deals. They will never be 'on offer', and beware of market stall fakes, at much lower prices, which are highly illegal. The luxury-products market never seems to suffer from reduced consumer spending.

Sales promotions may produce extra immediate receipts, but is the extra cost in terms of special publicity and merchandising material worth the hassle? Should they be considered as part of a medium- to long-term marketing plan for customer *fidélisation*? If you are retailing to a mainly French public, shop décor and ambience are also particularly important. Terence Conran, the founder of Habitat, was heavily influenced by the French way to retail. Also, IKEA, the Swedish furniture retailers, have very successfully opened up out-of-town hypermarkets catering for the French consumers' drive, buy and take-away habits. IKEA stores' easy floor layouts, convenient flat packs and well-designed furniture with clean lines for modern French homes, plus cafeterias serving Swedish food with food mini-markets (*superettes*), cater for customers throughout the buying process. On a much smaller retail scale, offering free coffee to retain potential customers is rare in France (for example in furniture shops, car showrooms, estate agents, etc.) and is perhaps something that could be developed. Discreet air-conditioning for comfort is increasing with longer, warmer seasons.

Retailing a typically British product in a British décor may need the expertise of an interior shop designer (*ensemblier*) to modify or adapt the scheme to one acceptable to the French public. Gift wrapping for presents in boutiques is standard practice and should not be overlooked as a customer service. In the property field, the American Real Estate Agents, Century 21, true to their name led the way in France in the 1990s with pro-active, effective imported marketing methods. They established a brand image for their franchisees as well-organised businesses selling properties fast at the right price. The American demijohn system dispensing chilled water in workplaces is another, more recent, example of a successful imported idea.

Membership of trade and professional associations will help if the product is sold to retailers or wholesalers. At the retail end, *NF* (*norme française*) standards label stuck onto articles or their packaging is not obligatory, but 90 per cent of French people will be reassured by it. While a 'made in France' label is no longer possible for many goods which are now imported from South-East Asia, *NF* means that products have been tested and factories inspected for quality, safety and suitability for customers' needs. Holiday businesses and travel companies increasingly use the label to certify approved safety conditions. Visit the English sections of the *NF* website for further information: www.marque-nf.com.

Free publicity is always acceptable provided it is in a medium that will be seen or read by at least part of the targeted market. Monthly community magazines which are delivered free to all householders' letter boxes often have a New Businesses page, written in a service-to-the-community editorial style. The write-up is free and the Editor of the magazine, who is probably the mayor, should be contacted for further information. Clever PR or press releases can also lead to free write-ups about your product and new organisations in business sections of the local and regional press. Independent reviews posted on your website or on wholesalers' and major distributors' websites with online shopping possibility can be very effective and won't cost a euro.

House letter boxes in France are easily accessible for posting publicity material. Modern ones are spacious, but, from an individual business' point of view, unfortunately encourage a host of regular publicity material. Individual letter boxes in blocks of flats tend to be smaller and are grouped together making publicity distribution quicker. If the business' market is local, messages can be distributed regularly, quickly and economically. A white non-addressed envelope containing a colour publicity, announcement or launch message will stand out and has a good chance of being opened and read.

Alternatively you could buy a display advertisement panel in the local tourist office/Chamber of Commerce/Municipal free street map and/or produce a New Year card or, better still, a calendar showing what you do for potential customers. This may also remind existing customers of your business. New Year greetings are an important social, political and business custom. Distribute the card or calendar, with a bit of leg work, through letter boxes or by reduced rate postage.

Advertising in specialised magazines for practical and semi-technical products to reach a clearly defined audience should not be overlooked. France publishes considerably more magazines in breadth and depth than the UK. If a substantial part of the market is English-speaking expatriates, display ads for image building and/or classified ads for general information, contact details and mail order possibilities can be placed in the following English language newspapers and magazines:

French News, SARL Brussac, 225 route d'Angoulème, BP 4042, 24004 Perigueux, France.

National/regional news, produced monthly, standard newsprint, in colour and black and white, tabloid with a print run of up to 60,000. See www.french-news.com for further information.

The Connexion, BP 25, 06480 La Colle sur Loup, France.

Mainly national news, printed monthly, standard newsprint in colour and black and white, a tabloid with a print run of around 30,000. See www.connexionfrance.com for further information.

The Riviera Times (incorporating *The Monaco Times*), 8 avenue Jean Moulin, 06340 Drap, France.

Mainly local news produced monthly, in glossy newsprint and colour throughout, a broadsheet with a print run of around 25,000. See www. rivieratimes.com for further information.

Property France (incorporating *Focus on France*), Outbound Publishing, 1 Commercial Road, Eastbourne, East Sussex, BN21 3XQ.

Property information and articles, produced every two months in glossy newsprint, colour throughout.
See www.outboundpublishing.com for further information.

French Property News, 6, Burgess Mews, Wimbledon, London SW19 1UF.

Property information and articles, produced monthly in glossy newsprint, colour throughout, has a circulation of around 50,000. See www.french-property-news.com for further information.

Pro-active marketing to British people through individually addressed mail shots to British names in the phone directory, especially if a free sample is enclosed, can be effective.

If your business is in the Côte d'Azur area advertise in the *Yellow Pages* directory, in English, as an English speaking business. Visit www.theanglophonebook.com for further information. On a national basis, if you offer a building service – from architects to swimming pool maintenance – post details in English on the www.artisan-anglais.com website.

WEBSITES

Creating a website provides a vehicle for strategic promotions, on-going on-line orders, informing customers of product range and new developments, answering questions and queries and mail shots which are either independent of or complementary to orthodox postal campaigns and phone canvassing. A web designer should be used who is also a professional copywriter in French with an understanding of French culture, customs and mentality. This is particularly useful for anticipating frequently asked questions from surfers and building up a list of questions and answers for insertion to the site. Once the site is created it can be easily updated if you are computer literate. You should ensure that the web designer's work is professional and visit websites they have constructed. It is astounding how many poorly constructed sites exist with difficult-to-read descriptions on poorly contrasted backgrounds and, in addition, are not easy for locating information. Don't forget to protect the name of your French website, i.e. those that end in '.fr', by registering it with the *AFNIC* (*Association française pour le Nommage Internet en Coopération*) on www.afnic.asso.fr.

On-line debit card transactions are becoming increasingly important in France. Broadband (*ADSL*) is widespread – about 50 per cent of French households now have the Internet – enabling subscribers to receive and open email quickly and enjoy animated audiovisual messages. Bear in mind that although the 2004 *LEN* law (*loi pour la confiance dans l'économie numérique*) encourages Internet business transactions it forbids *unsolicited* email publicity. Potential customers who have agreed to be on address lists which are sold to businesses for postal publicity may not have agreed to receive email publicity. Existing and new on-line customers can however (and should from a business point of view) be solicited with publicity and offers for similar goods and services '*produits et services analogues*'. Website offers are, of course, not unsolicited as the surfer decides whether or not to visit the site and its links.

With unlimited time part of broadband contracts, email unit cost is miniscule. Even on a pay-as-you-use basis email only costs about 1/6th of the cost of post. It is the same price to anywhere in the world meaning that wider and/or more frequent campaigns are possible and it provides almost instant insight into what the competition are up to. Results can be judged quickly as response is rapid and interest in website offers and individual links can be estimated as visits to webs and their links are automatically recorded by computer technology. The Internet is a powerful marketing tool – don't get caught out with unprecedented on-line demand which cannot be fulfilled. Reputations, particularly in the early days of a business, will never be made if promised delivery periods are not met. Sales promotions for gifts for Easter, Mother's Day, Christmas Day, etc., must live up to delivery promises or cover themselves 'subject to stock' or with an automatic computer-generated block on further orders. Offer delivery periods you know you can beat – Anglo-Saxon reliability impresses French customers.

PROSPECTING AND GETTING APPOINTMENTS

All businesses which sell to or trade with other businesses must find time on a regular basis to seek out and meet new potential customers to replace existing business and contracts which, for a variety of reasons, go elsewhere or drop off. This requires disciplined organisation for small businesses which cannot justify staff, even on a part-time basis, or even use commission-only outside representation to do this. The one-man band should diarise set times and stick to them. Monday mornings and Friday afternoons are often staff meeting times in small companies and should be avoided as the buyer or boss to be contacted will be otherwise involved.

Cold-calling for a business-to-business activity such as office supplies or cleaning products, operating locally, can be very effective; especially if a practical demonstration is made immediately or by appointment. In my experience, being a foreigner is a positive advantage for being well received as you will stand out from French callers.

Writing or phoning for appointments is more difficult. Two methods, however, have a good success rate.

1. An initial letter briefly presenting the product or service in terms of advantages (cost savings, flexibility, etc.) for the company concerned. This requires some research and should be addressed, ideally to the company manager or the buyer. The letter should terminate with the announcement that the addressee will be contacted in the next few days for an appointment.

2. Phone and give your name – pronounce it slowly or spell it out – and ask to be put through to the person concerned. If you don't sound French and have a distinctly Anglo-Saxon name you are at an advantage. Then, if and when you are put through, outline why you are phoning for an appointment and ask for one.

Following up initial-approach letters is when you may encounter the barrier put up by the switchboard or a high-powered management secretary (*secrétaire de direction*), depending on the size of the company. Explain clearly to whoever answers the phone that you are phoning to contact *Monsieur* or *Madame* (give specific name) regarding the letter to them. With small companies try phoning at the end of the day, just after normal office hours, when you may get through directly to the person wanted. They may also be more relaxed and receptive, winding down from a busy day.

The appointment risk with small business prospects is that the manager you have arranged to see will be involved with an unexpected problem or delayed because they have had to go and see someone elsewhere on urgent business. Dealing with works committees (*comités d'entreprise (CE)*) on the other hand can be comparatively straightforward and involve big business. All companies employing at least 50 people must have a *CE*, whose elected committee members manage the annual budget. The committee members have fixed times for visits and an office or special area to look at offers for the staff ranging from camping holidays to yoga lessons.

USEFUL VOCABULARY

cible	target
courriel (although the words 'email' and 'mail' are widely used in correspondence and everyday language, the term '*courriel*' is used sometimes in official papers and texts)	email
entreprise de routage	mailing company
marketing sensorial	sensory marketing
marketing générationnel	vertical marketing to successive age groups
promotion de produits en plus	special packs
service après-vente (SAV)	after-sales service
télé-marketing	phone canvassing
tendances	market trends
vente par correspondance (VPC)	mail order

12

Employing people

Has development of the business reached the point where maintaining production and customers or increasing turnover now requires staff? Perhaps you should consider carefully whether to take on salaried staff full-time or part-time or for a limited period. Full-time staff needs serious consideration as social security contributions for the employer represent a high percentage of salary. Trainees or apprentices under the various government schemes described further below may be the solution. Upgrading your computers so that they are more beneficial to the business might also be a solution and cheaper than employing new staff. If new customers are needed, perhaps an independent, self-employed agent (*agent commercial*) is the immediate solution.

Before making a choice, understand how the heavily regulated and costly employment process, the French continental system, works. Whilst plenty of people are looking for work – almost 10 per cent of the available workforce is looking for jobs, with just over 20 per cent in the under-25 age group, just under 50 per cent in the 55 to 59 pre-retirement age group unemployed, and 37 per cent in the 55 to 64 age group – employment law can make hiring and firing difficult. Employers' social security contributions, especially for executives who are reluctant to forego the *cadre* status, are so high that in practice the creation of new jobs is slowed right down or even prevented. Employees in French companies cost their employers almost twice the amount of their salary cheque.

The choice of employment contracts is perhaps too wide and therefore confusing, with new options being introduced to aid first-time employers and encourage first-time employees all too regularly. At the beginning of 2006 there were 12 measures aimed at helping various categories of the unemployed back into employment. Effective solutions have yet to be found. It is becoming almost commonplace for successive governments to test-market new ideas or employment contracts in a limited geographical area before deciding whether or not to launch them nationally.

RECRUITMENT
Announcing the post

Establishing contacts or networking to produce recommended candidates from people you know who understand you, the way the business works and your requirements, should be an important part of your recruitment campaign. Statistics claim that 75 per cent of all jobs are not advertised. Apart from *Certificats de travail* which confirm with sound French logic that candidates have worked with the employer(s) detailed on their CV for the period mentioned, written references are scarce. Don't hesitate to ask to see *Certificats de travail* when interviewing, provided candidates have been forewarned to bring them.

Traditional means such as classified or display advertisements in newspapers and specialised trade press, not forgetting freely distributed press with cheaper advertising rates, and announcements which will be prepared by the local Job Centre (*ANPE*) and executive Job Centres (*APEC*), are of course still essential. *L'Express*, *Le Point* and the *Courrier Cadres* (the latter is published by *APEC* with appointments categorised in 12 groups) weekly magazines carry advertisements for managerial appointments, and Job Centre announcements are increasingly consulted online (www.anpe.fr and www.apec.fr).

Advertisements should contain or ask for the following basic information:

♦ The company's business address for postal candidatures, size, market sector and position, and operating area.
♦ A brief description of vacant or new positions, job title, start date, type of contract, salary range, training, hours/conditions, potential.
♦ Candidates' employment experience, languages, professional training/educational certificates/diplomas, age and motivation.

A typical Job Centre *cadre* announcement in a standardised form could read as overleaf. The announcement is from a small company seeking an English-speaking international business developer of technical product sales, who will be working via the Internet.

In this example candidates will reply directly. Bear in mind if you are discussing your requirements with a Job Centre placement consultant that consultants are unlikely to have any real knowledge of your type of business as most of them are career civil servants and will not have had outside employment experience. There is also increasing pressure from the government to reduced

Offre No ....
Ets de: 5 salariés   Secteur: études techniques
Recherche pour un contrat à durée indéterminée
Chargé(e) de développent commercial international H/F
Lieu ....
Horaires: 35 h hebdomadaire

Pour leader dans le domaine de la communication sur Internet
(65 per cent du c.a. à l'export). En collaboration avec l'équipe
technique: prospection, développement et fidélisation du
portefeuille à l'international. Responsable commercial et mar-
keting.

Formation: BTS.
Produits: industriels au niveau mondial
Connaissances: langue anglaise exigée
Expérience exigée de 01 an minimum à l'étranger.

Salaire mensuel indicatif de 2300,00€
Envoyer votre CV et lettre de motivation manuscrite à ....
..

the unemployment figures, so many candidates who do not have suitable experience or potential are now pushed forward by Job Centres. The *ANPE* and privately-run recruitment consultants no longer have the monopoly on offering permanent jobs. Temporary-job organisations such as Manpower and Adecco now also handle them.

Curriculum Vitae and interviews

CVs fall into three basic categories as outlined below.

The '*standard*', which applicants use to reply to all job advertisements without any modifications; the '*modulaire*' which highlights certain information which is particularly relevant to the post announced and the '*sur mesure*' – a custom-built model – which shows that the candidate has gone to some trouble to find out about your activity and your company's position in the market place and indicates how their employment experience can be immediately effective. The *CV anonyme* (anonymous CV) is the latest government experiment being tested for some jobs announced, and applied for, through Job Centres. While the anonymous CV may still be *standard*, *modulaire* or *sur mesure*, it deliberately does not show the age or surname of the candidate or contain their photograph, on the grounds that many employers automatically reject candidatures because of age, race or national origins.

A CV of just one page is usual, with career (*parcours professionnel*) set out in reverse chronological order, possibly preceded by a skills (*compétences*) section which will be particularly important in '*sur mesure*' CVs, and terminating with education and professional training/diplomas (*formation/instruction*) and proficiency in any languages. Applicants applying for their first clerical or administrative job, without any previous experience, know that they are expected to have passed, at the very least, the *baccalauréat* (school leaving examination for 18-year-olds). An up-to-date photo as well as the age of candidates are, with the exception of the 'anonymous CV' also usual, accompanied by a hand-written (unless email applications are permitted) letter of motivation. This letter is an important part of the candidate's application setting out why they feel your business needs them: much more than just a covering letter.

The business and the position concerned can be presented to a group of previously selected candidates or following a general advertisement in the press of the business' presentation. Time will thus be saved on presentation to all candidates who are interviewed, or who decide to confirm their interest and stay for an interview. If this method is chosen ask each candidate to fill in an application form on-the-spot which can then be checked against their previously posted or emailed CV. This system is often used for taking on staff who will be representing the business outside the main office and possibly some distance away from it. The venue will usually be in a specially hired room. Candidates' interview travelling expenses will not have to be paid. As a general rule in France travel expenses for interviews are not offered, even for pre-arranged individual interviews for management appointments, unless a journey of over 200 kilometres is necessary.

Some obvious points which should not be overlooked, when employing French staff with whom you will be working closely are to ensure that you, literally, understand each other and that they know precisely what is expected of them. See *Some False Friends*, Appendix 2. Apart from understanding different temperaments and backgrounds, any potentially disastrous Fawlty Towers situations will be avoided!

Consider the following questions as well:

- Would you be happy as a customer if they were presenting the product or service to you?
- Do they create a good first impression?
- Do they speak frankly about any grey areas in their CV?

Correct use of the informal *tu* and *toi* (*tutoiement*) and formal *vous* (*vouvoiement*) second person singular pronouns should not be overlooked, when speaking or writing to French staff. In fact, there are no hard and fast rules, so it is important to understand the basic principles so that the use of *tu* or *vous* becomes automatic in appropriate circumstances. From a boss' point of view always being addressed as *vous* ensures that respect is maintained and working relationships are kept on a businesslike level. Using Christian names is becoming increasingly customary at work between colleagues with similar or different levels of responsibility, and does not necessarily open the way for *tu* and *toi*. If in doubt stick to *vous*.

Salaries

These are announced in advertisements as monthly or annual. Salaries for executive appointments are nearly always announced as annual, but conversation is nearly always about how much a *month* the job pays net. Salary packages are 100 per cent basic (*fixe*), or composed of a high basic salary (*salaire de base*) and a variable and usually lower, personal or company performance-related annual bonus or monthly commission (*variable/intéressement*). Annual bonuses (*primes annuelles*) are increasingly used and apart from encouraging extra effort from employees can be offset against *IS* (corporation) tax. Bonuses classed as one-offs (*primes exceptionnelles*) are also free of social security contributions for both employer and employee as they are not considered as regular remuneration.

Commission-only salaried positions also exist, or low-basic salaried positions with high commission potential, notably with estate agencies as income cannot be immediately generated.

Salary levels are slightly lower than in the UK, although any truly bilingual English and French speaking person in a responsible position can expect to be well paid. Paris and the Ile de France area pay up to 10 per cent more than the rest of France. Current salary rates can be checked on the website www.infosalaire.fr, and *L'Express* and *Courrier Cadres* magazines publish salary ranges covering the whole spectrum of managerial positions at least once a year. *L'Entreprise* magazine (www.lentreprise.com), in collaboration with the Expectra recruitment organisation, published a survey in September 2005 of average managerial salaries throughout France in small- and medium-sized businesses, with separate figures for the Paris/Ile de France area. They surveyed 115 different types of jobs. Company cars (*voitures de fonction*) are not as common as in the UK, although generous mileage allowances can be claimed against personal taxation by employees who have to use their own car to travel to and from their work. In the Paris area employers subsidise 50 per cent of the cost of employees' public transport season tickets. Elsewhere, reasonably priced public transport season tickets, which are not subsidised by employers, are valid on working days for employees. The application for season tickets must be signed and stamped by the employer.

The national minimum salary, the *SMIC*, is revised every year in July. At present it is just over 1,300€ a month gross (*brut*) for adults working a 35-hour week. From a small business' point of view, it saves a lot of trouble, and possibly money, in deciding or negotiating a starting salary with relatively inexperienced staff.

Assuming that you are employing French staff and that the salary is negotiable you may need to bring in a French consultant. The consultant will know better than you how to pinpoint what the successful candidate will really accept and how best to conclude a satisfactory deal for you without burning any cultural bridges. Ensure that your consultant is quite clear as to the maximum monthly or annual gross (*brut*) salary you are prepared to pay.

Businesses with five employees or fewer, except those with salaried farm-workers, can join the *service chèque-emploi centre* to simplify salary payments. The initial registration of the salaried employee with the *centre* using the on-line declaration form (*déclaration unique emploi*) can also serve as the employment contract. Every month the *centre* will make up employee(s) salary slips and send details of the social security payments due from the business. Registration can be made online at www.emploi.tpe.fr. If the business has more than five employees, salary slips can be prepared by this organisation for any additional occasional staff.

All salary slips show the following :

♦ The name and address of both the company and the employee.
♦ The month concerned and the date of payment. (The latter may be a few days after the end of the month if cheques from customers taken into account for commission payments have to be cleared.)
♦ The company's 14-figure *siret* business registration number. *NAF* (*nomenclature d'activités françaises*) business classification number. *URSSAF* branch office and company number.
♦ The employee's job title, social security number, and commencement of employment date.
♦ The number of hours worked in the month. (This will not necessarily be a true reflection of the actual hours worked by a

conscientious *cadre*.) The month's gross fixed salary with any commission shown separately followed by total gross salary. The various payments to *URSSAF*, pension funds, the national unemployment benefit fund and other social funds are then detailed separately. Businesses with under 10 staff can pay every three months, by the 15th of the month: for example 15th January, 15th April, 15th July and 15th October. Note that if the business uses the more convenient direct debit system proposed by the *service chèque-emploi centre*, payments will in effect be made approximately every two months. Employer and employee contributions and respective percentages of total gross salary are shown under the headings :

maladie (for sickness, maternity, and death benefits)

accidents (for accident/invalidity benefit)

veuvage (for widows benefit)

familiale (family allowance)

vieillesse (basic pension)

FNA logement (national housing assistance fund)

assedic (chomage) (for unemployment benefit)

retraite complémentaire (standard complementary pension. *Cadres* must contribute in addition to another pension scheme)

CSG (supplementary social security contribution in aid of the underprivileged)

◆ Net taxable income total, followed by: deductions of *RDS* (social security deficit-repayment fund contribution) and a larger *CSG* amount which cannot be claimed against tax by employees, and then the 'bottom line' take-home pay amount (*net à payer*).

Employers contribute to all funds except *veuvage*, the *CSG* and the *RDS*. Despite these exceptions, employers' total contribution amount (*charges patronales*) to all relevant categories is about double full-time employees' total contributions (*charges salariales*). The latter total around 25 per cent of gross salary. Both totals must be shown *and* the total contribution amount (*charges*) paid by the business, i.e. *charges patronales* plus *charges salariales*. Employers also pay into a national training fund for employees, with companies already employing 10 or more staff paying a greater percentage of salary than smaller companies. Businesses employing nine people which were hesitant about employing a tenth person, because it increased *charges*, now benefit from a government reduction in these contributions. This reduction applies to all businesses now taking on up to and including 19 salaried employees.

Payment method (cheque or bank transfer) and the cumulative number of hours worked since the beginning of the calendar year should also be shown, as well as remaining holiday entitlement (see Employment Conditions below).

EMPLOYMENT CONDITIONS
Holiday entitlement
The 35-hour week, probably the shortest official working week in the world for full-time employees, is now more flexible and employers may offer up to an additional 220 hours a year to employees. Employees are not however obliged to accept longer hours. This is a point to discuss with job candidates who are interviewed. Working hours must be displayed on the premises.

All employees are entitled to five weeks paid holiday (30 working days) annually based on their usual income. The holiday year for most categories of business runs from 1 June to 31 May and entitlement to the full five weeks, strictly speaking, is only reached when a complete holiday year has been worked. In practice, arrangements can usually be made with employees to ensure they don't miss out on five weeks in any holiday year. Employees cannot be made to take holidays outside the official holiday season (*période légale*) running from 1st May to 31st October, but both bosses and employees are usually happy to accept at least a week's holiday over Christmas. In fact, many manufacturing and service businesses now close down from Christmas Eve to the 2nd of January. Not many employees take four weeks' holiday in one go, although the legal entitlement still exists. Employees are paid for all public holidays and the month of May is shot through with them, with Labour Day (*Fête du travail*) and VE day, and often Ascension Day. With the shorter working week and any public holidays falling on a Thursday or Tuesday (Ascension Day is always on a Thursday) staff may ask for extended weekends with intervening normal working days deducted from their 30-day holiday entitlement. Whit Monday is no longer a public holiday.

Medical benefits

A free medical check-up is obligatory for all employees once a year. If your premises are not near a *Médecin du Travail* surgery a fully-equipped van with at least one doctor and nurse will announce its forthcoming visit to the locality for you and other businesses, and employees will be given due notice of the time and date for their 20-minute visit. The medical results will confirm whether or not the employee is fit (*apt*) to start or continue the duties their work demands. It is a condition of confirmed employment that a future employee has a check-up for *aptitude* just before or after the employment contract is signed.

Maternity benefits

Maternity leave (*congé de maternité*) for employees, if requested, is obligatory on full pay with employment held over. Even the smallest companies, where this may create a staffing problem, are included. For the first or second child a total of 16 weeks is given: six before the due date and 10 after. From the third child onwards leave is extended to 24 weeks. The entitlement for twins is 34 weeks and for triplets or more, 46 weeks' leave is permitted. Absence for medical examinations and limited extensions on production of a doctor's certificates, are permitted without loss of pay. Fathers are entitled to two weeks' paternity leave or three weeks for twins, triplets on 80 per cent of gross salary, limited to around 840€ a month.

Salaried employees who have worked in the same company for at least 12 months when the child is born are entitled to unpaid extended post-natal maternity, or paternity, leave (*congé paternal d'éducation*) with their full-time job held over for them. Under certain conditions, this also applies to part-time employees. This continuous leave can be extended until the child is three years old.

Smoking at work

Smoking is banned at work if there are non-smokers employed by the business. This law is not always applied in small businesses if the majority of staff are smokers. Large businesses with office staff and non-production line workers often tolerate a quick cigarette break in working time just off the premises.

Air conditioning and water facilities

Premises must be adequately aerated: at least 7 m³ of air per employee, and in laboratories, kitchens, and shops and offices open to the public at least 10 m³ of air per employee. Cold, not more than 15° centigrade, drinking water must be available for staff. There should be sufficient hot- and cold-water hand-wash basin(s) depending on staff numbers – at least one for 10 people.

Works committees

Companies employing at least 50 people should have a works committee (*comité d'entreprises*). One of its roles being to represent staff requests or grievances with management. Companies of this size must also have a hygiene, safety and conditions of work committee (*CHSCT*). Smaller companies, with at least 11 employees, have a staff representative (*délégué du personnel*). Employers are entitled to suspend salary if an employee strikes, unless it is subsequently ruled – in the case of individual employees, by the *Prud'hommes* industrial tribunal – that the employee's grievance was justified: for example, working conditions which do not respect security regulations. A refectory must be provided if at least 25 salaried people request it, and in theory a room should be set aside for lunch breaks in all smaller companies. Precise lunch break times can be written into employment contracts, provided they do not contravene any collective labour agreements. See Employment contracts below. The minimum (Dickensian) requirement for a break under employment law is at least 20 minutes every 6 hours. In practice employers are more generous than that. Any time not worked is, of course, not paid for.

EMPLOYMENT BENEFITS

The four optional benefits described below should only be considered for full-time employees. A lot of small businesses do not offer them as they feel they are too costly.

Le treizième mois

This is an end-of-year extra month's salary or bonus payment which is often offered by large financial organisations to their employees.

Mutuelle health insurance

As social security health cover in France is only partial, with 70 per cent of the cost of GP visits and 80 per cent of hospital in-patient costs (without any surgical operation) paid by the health service, a top-up health insurance cover with a *mutuelle* company may be a benefit requested by a future key member of full-time staff. A 50/50 share between employee and employer is not unreasonable if membership of a *mutuelle* is negotiated as part of the employment contract.

Chéques vacances

These benefit employees on low salaries by allowing them to save up for coupons which can be used for holiday travel and accommodation purposes within France. The employer who has opted for the scheme must contribute at least 20 per cent to the cost of the coupons which have a value of 25 per cent more than the amount saved by the employee.

Titres de restaurants (luncheon vouchers)

Employers pay between 50 and 60 per cent of their cost.

EMPLOYMENT CONTRACTS

Employment law in France covering hiring (and firing) employees is detailed in the annually updated *Code du Travail* tome, found in the business section of any good bookshop. So, with this useful book available, there is no excuse for not knowing employees rights. At least employers can consult the extensive regulations and official procedures rapidly and make sure that any areas of possible future disagreement, which would tend to be judged in favour of employees, are reduced as much as possible.

CDD, CDI and *CNE* contracts

All employment contracts are either *contrat à durée déterminée* (*CDD*) or *contrat à durée indéterminée* (*CDI*). Contracts with French registered companies must of course be written in French throughout. English words such as 'top' and 'look' which are used conversationally are invalid, whilst words like 'weekend' which have been officially part of the French language for many years can be used.

The *CDD* is a fixed period contract which must be put in writing. It should contain the following elements:

♦ Names and addresses of both the employing company and the employee, with company registration number and employee's social security number, preceded by *Entre les soussignés*;

♦ Introduction to what has been decided and agreed (*Il a donc été arrêté et convenu ce qui suit*);

♦ Clauses (*articles*) specifying period and hours to be worked, the job description (*poste occupé, définitions des missions confiées*), remuneration, and asserting that professional confidentiality must be kept during the *CDD*. A clause preventing the employee from working afterwards for a competitor (*article de non-concurrence*) is no longer valid;

◆ If conditions, which may be lengthy, of the collective labour agreement (*convention collective*) covering the type of business (*NAF*) are not detailed in the contract, the employer should cover themselves by asking the employee to accept the *convention* conditions using a sentence such as: *Pour toutes les dispositions non-prévues au present contrat, les parties déclarent se référer à la convention collective dont dépend la société.* For example, cafés, hotels and restaurants – known collectively as *CHR* – share the same agreement.

The contract should be drawn up in duplicate with both examples dated and signed at the end of the last page by the employer and employee with the company's location specified next to the date. The employer should sign over their company stamp and the employee's name should be typed out for signature and preceded by their hand written agreement '*Bon pour accord*' or '*Lu et approuvé*'. Pages preceding the last page should be initialled in the margin by both parties.

Other than its application in contracts for young adults, the registered unemployed and the pre-retirement contract described further below, a *CDD* contract can only be used to replace an employee temporarily, such as maternity leave, and to help meet a temporary upsurge in business activity following, for example, the award of a large business contract or during peak seasons in the *CHR* and tourism trades. It can only normally last for an overall period of 18 months which includes any renewal periods, otherwise the employee must be taken on permanently. As it is a fixed period contract it can only be terminated before the end-of-contract date by mutual agreement between employer and employee, or in *force majeure* circumstances. The employee can be sacked in the case of professional misconduct such as embezzlement or theft. If the employee finds permanent employment elsewhere they can break the *CDD* contract by giving up to two weeks' notice.

The *CDI* is considered as permanent employment as no fixed period is specified and is usually subject to a probationary period of up to three months during which time no notice to break the contract is required by employer or employee. After this period the usual redundancy or termination of employment regulations (see page 195) apply. It is advisable to draw up a written contract, although this is not obligatory if a full-time employee is taken on. Think very carefully before employing someone with a *CDI* contract. Once past the three-month trial period it is almost impossible to replace someone if they fall into an acceptable, but never improving, rut.

The *contrat nouvelle embauche* (*CNE*) is a new (introduced in 2005) employment contract considered as a *CDI*, but with an initial two-year trial period. It is applicable to small- and medium-size businesses with no more than 20 staff. A written contract is obligatory. It gives developing companies, which may encounter unforeseen problems, flexibility to lay-off staff without any justification during this initial period, simply by sending a recorded-delivery letter of notice. Two weeks' notice is required between two and six months of starting the *CNE* and one month thereafter. If business picks up the same employee can be taken on again after three months with a new *CNE* contract. The restrictions for employers imposed by *CDD*s and standard *CDI*s are therefore avoided. This can be a good contract to use for small new businesses, particularly those owned and run by foreigners, if they are unsure if they will need someone long term or are inexperienced in assessing the real qualities of French candidates.

Special contracts for young adults

The *contrat d'apprentissage* is a fixed period sandwich course contract for apprentices between the ages of 16 and 25 and lasts from one to three years. It can be a useful means for an employer to develop the potential of a school leaver with future long-term employment in their business in mind. The salary paid to the apprentice is based on the national minimum salary and varies according to age and the professional exam that is being studied for. The apprentice must go to a training centre (*centre de formation*) for at least 400 hours a year.

The *contrat jeune en entreprise* (*CJE*) contract is an unlimited-period contract designed to encourage the employment of people in the 16- to 23-year-old age group who left school without taking the *baccalauréat* exam and also those in the 16- to 26-year-old age group who have no educational qualifications at all. The contract can be for full-time or part-time employment and the corresponding salary must at least equal the pro-rata amount of the national minimum salary for the number of hours worked. Government financial incentive is substantial for the employer, who receives either 150 or 300 euros a month depending on the educational level of the employee for a period of two years, and then 50 per cent in the third year which is paid quarterly. Part-time, which must be at least half of the full-time hours, *CJE* employees entitle their employer to a pro-rata amount of the appropriate (150 or 300 euros) amount. *Charges patronales* social security contributions are also reduced.

The *contrat de professionalisation* contract is either a limited period contract, usually for six or 12 months, or an unlimited period contract. It is designed for all adults up to the age of 26, and also the unemployed who are over 26, who require a professional qualification to help their future employment prospects. It provides professional training in a *centre de formation* of between 150 and 260 hours, and sometimes more in exceptional circumstances, and a qualification which is usually closely linked to the specific activity of the employer. Salary is based on effective working hours in the enterprise and also depends on age if candidates are under 26. Employers use it to mould future full-time employees to the requirements of their business.

These three contracts should not be confused with unpaid higher education students who are accepted by businesses as part of their academic course onto a non-productive, training or observational basis as *stagiaires*. Beware of the temptation to pay full-time students who are occasional *stagiaires* for work on a non-salaried, and therefore illegal basis. *CIDJ* (*Centre information de la jeunesse*) careers advisory centre offices recommend a written agreement outlining the in-company study programme and duration for *stagiaires*. Since January 2006 all *stagiares* remaining more than three months with a business must be paid a salary.

Pre-retirement contract for the unemployed

This recent contract is for those over the age of 57, who have been registered for at least three months as unemployed and looking for their final job to take them up to the normal retirement age of 60. Employers requiring an experienced person at a reasonable price for a medium-term assignment will be attracted by it. The contract is in fact a *CDD* for a maximum period of 18 months which can be renewed once more for the period initially contracted.

Other contracts for the unemployed

Employers taking on employees under *CIE* and *CI-RMA* contracts have financial advantages.

The *contrat intiative emploi* (*CIE*) contract is either a *CDI* or a *CDD* lasting from 12 to 24 months on a full-time or part-time basis of at least 17.0 hours per week. It is designed to help the long-term unemployed back into employment as the government subsidise their salary. Provided an agreement is signed with the *ANPE* the employer is entitled to a monthly government cheque, paid in advance, amounting to up to 47 per cent of the national minimum hourly wage. The actual amount depends on the type and legal form of the business and its location. In addition the employer is exempted to the tune of 26 per cent of the national minimum hourly wage of the *charges patronales* social security contributions they would normally pay.

The *contrat d'insertion-revenu minimum d'activité* (*CI-RMA*) is a *CDD* on a full-time or part-time basis of at least 20 hours a week. It is reserved for people on social security and the salary paid must equal the national minimum hourly wage rate for the number of hours worked. The salary is subsidised by the government who pay the employer 425.40€ a month in advance. The contract is signed either with the *Conseil Général* (County Council) or the *ANPE* depending on the type of social security the candidate receives. In addition the employer is exempted from *charges patronales* social security contributions similar to those for the *CIE*.

Part-time contracts

If just a few hours a week extra help is required, an employer contributes 30 per cent less to *charges patronales* for social security, accidents at work and family allowances, subject to the following conditions:

- The hours worked must be less than one fifth of the legal working week. (This is ideal for businesses that have particularly busy periods after normal office hours; after the weekend on Monday mornings; Saturday mornings; during staff holiday periods, etc.)
- A written contract either for *CDD* or *CDI* employment. (Businesses with under 11 staff, with no *délégué du personnel*, just have to advise the employment inspectorate (*l'inspection du travail*) at the *Direction Départementale du Travail* (*DDT*) office.)

If an applicant for part-time employment is salaried elsewhere for at least four fifths of the legal working week, it may not be necessary to pay any *charges sociales* for them at all, provided they agree to this. Check the position with the *DDT* showing proof of their employment elsewhere with their working hours.

Portage salarial contract

This recent concept solves the problem of finding experienced salaried executives for part-time work (which is usually half of the working week hours), either long or short term, instead of on a full-time basis which would be too costly for the business. *Portage salarial* cannot be used for manual workers. It is a tripartite system. The person working for you is employed by an administrative organisation that pays their salary and social security contributions and which invoices your business for an amount which includes the total employment cost and a service fee of around 10 per cent. The *portage salarial* 'employee' is available because they can complete a full working week elsewhere with another contract managed by their administrative organisation. Visit www.portagesalariale.org for further details and a list of national federation members.

Agent commercial

If representation to sales outlets for immediate results is required, consider appointing a commission-only sales agent (*agent commercial*). Your business will not have to bear the cost of any sales prospecting which does not produce any orders. An experienced *agent* will know the territory, have a good relationship with their existing customers and know which ones to contact for new and future business, and generally be able to gain acceptance from the trade for a fresh product.

Sales agents calling on wholesalers and retailers will expect a commission rate of up to around 15 per cent calculated on trade invoice amounts, exclusive of VAT (*HT*). The rate of commission will depend on the unit value of the product(s), the size of the territory and the call cycle required. While trade sales agents remain independent and usually represent several businesses, property sales agents are usually attached to just one estate agency business as if they were a salaried employee although they are free, unlike salaried employees, to organise their work as they see fit. Property sales agents receive up to 50 per cent of the commission on a property sale received by the estate agency if they have both found and sold the property; and up to 25 per cent of the estate agency's commission if they just find *or* sell the property.

Contracts with all agents should contain the following elements:

◆ Names and addresses of the principal and the agent, with the principal's registration number, preceded by *Entré les soussignés*;

◆ Introduction to what has been decided and agreed (*Il a donc été arrêté et convenu ce qui suit*);

◆ Clauses (*articles*) confirming that the contract cannot be considered as an employment contract subject to employment legislation (*Code du travail*); that the agent will produce (within a specified time) proof that they are registered as an *agent commercial* with their local Tribunal de Commerce and are also registered for obligatory contributions to social security organisations (*caisses sociales*); that the principal mandates the agent to represent their business and that the agent promises professional confidentiality; the territory concerned (*lieu d'activité*) – with property sales there is usually no limit – and the duration of the contract. The duration may be open-ended like a *CDI* for estate agency work with increasing periods of notice the longer the contract runs, or subject to review, after one year, for trade sales agents.

◆ The Commission rate for the agent and conditions of sale and prices should be separate clauses. The right to negotiate prices with, or without, prior referral to the principal should be specified. With trade sales agents contracts it is usual that the agent can take new customer contacts with him, but not business *contracts*, if the contract between the principal and agent is terminated. This is an important point to consider before signing an *agent commercial* contract. While agents are free to accept other representation contracts (*cartes*), a *fidélité* clause should be a condition of any contract, preventing agents from representing a competing business.

Contracts should be approved, signed and dated as with salaried employment contracts. It is sensible to draw them up in triplicate with one example being sent to the registrar (*greffe*) at the Tribunal de Commerce concerned.

EMPLOYING HUSBANDS OR WIVES

Regardless of the legal form of the business a husband or wife (*conjoint*) can be a salaried employee like anyone else with most of the tax advantages and social security benefits enjoyed by all salaried employees. NB: at the time of writing the French authorities' position regarding the UK's December 2005 Civil Partnership Act was unclear. A British civil partner setting up a business in France wishing to protect the other partner in the same way as a husband or wife who were married in the UK should check for any latest clarification with the British Embassy or Consulate office in France or with a specialised lawyer. Visit www.service-public.fr (the website is in English) for any updated information. If the business is a company which has opted for *IS* tax the salary of the *conjoint salarié* is accounted for in the usual way as a non-taxable pre-profit cost. If the business or company is taxed on a personal income (*IR*) basis the salary will also be a pre-profit cost, provided that the couple were married under the *séparation des biens* contract, meaning they are taxed separately. Couples married under the *communauté universelle* or *participation aux acquêts* agreements – described in Chapter 3 – may be entitled to considerable tax advantages provided the business belongs to a *CGA* or *AGA* accounts organisation.

Or if the business is an *EI* or *EURL* – farming excluded – and cannot afford to pay the *conjoint*, they can be covered as the *conjoint collaborateur* (colleague) by the entrepreneur's obligatory assurance for sickness, maternity and retirement pension. This retirement pension covers the basic and complementary systems for *artisans* and *commerçants* and just basic pension for the professions. A *conjoint collaborateur* can also work up to, but not more than, half the working week elsewhere in salaried employment, thus helping the business and gaining a regular income at the same time.

A third possibility of obtaining social security cover for a spouse is if he or she is a capital-holding partner in a company business. *SA* companies are excluded. As a salaried minor share-holder the spouse enjoys all of the social security benefits excluding unemployment cover.

REDUNDANCY (*LICENCIEMENT ÉCONOMIQUE*) AND DISMISSALS (*LICENCIEMENTS POUR MOTIF PERSONNEL*)

There is a set redundancy procedure which employers must follow. The former boss of Marks and Spencer was fined in 2005 by the French authorities for not following the correct procedure before Marks and Spencer withdrew from the French market in 2001. The procedure can vary, giving additional compensation and retraining opportunities for employees, depending on the *convention collective* for the type of employment. Earning better profits is not a valid reason for making employees redundant, but ensuring a company's survival by remaining competitive in the marketplace is. Remaining competitive may involve a change or pruning of the workforce following economic difficulties or technological advances in the business' speciality.

The procedure for a company with less than 50 employees, i.e. with no *comité d'entreprise*, is an initial instruction to attend an explanatory interview when the possibility of redundancy is mooted and any other employment opportunities within the company are discussed. The employee can be accompanied by the *délégué du personnel* who represents the staff's interests, or failing this, can choose to be accompanied by an official from a locally appointed independent 'redundancy' panel. If redundancy is the employer's only solution they must confirm this by registered letter to the employee. The obligatory period of paid notice can be worked, or not worked, at the employer's discretion. Two hours a day paid time of the employee's normal working day is allowed for prospecting for new employment.

The management of companies with at least 50 employees and planning to make at least 10 staff redundant must consider any solutions put forward by the *comité d'entreprise*, such as regrading, redeployment, outplacement, retraining, reduction of the working week, etc. Companies with over 1,000 employees, planning massive lay-offs, must provide a paid period of organised counselling and training (*congé de reclassement*) lasting several months.

The amount of redundancy payment depends on the number of years the employee has been continuously employed by the same company with a *CDI* contract and also on the *convention collective*. The payment includes outstanding holiday pay (*indemnité de congés-payés*) and any dismissal indemnities entitlement (*indemnité de licenciement*). The local *Direction Départementale du travail* office can confirm entitlement. All employees made redundant have priority in the first 12 months after redundancy for any new job opportunity, subject to any required training, with their former employer.

Temporary lay-off (*licenciement technique*), which may become permanent, can be applied immediately in *force majeure* circumstances which close down or hamper the business. This may include natural catastrophes, criminal damage, striking suppliers unable to deliver raw materials or parts, etc.

Employees can be dismissed for gross misconduct (*faute grave*), which includes theft and violence, and intentional gross misconduct (*faute lourde*), without any notice period or indemnities. *Faute lourde* may be difficult to prove so make sure grounds, such as often being late for work, not obeying work orders or not working at all, are well founded otherwise an industrial tribunal (*conseil des prud'hommes*) will give the benefit of the doubt to the employee. The basic procedure of a written notice (*convocation*) sent to the employee for an explanatory interview, followed by a recorded-delivery letter confirming any dismissal decision, must be followed if incompetence or unsatisfactory performance (*insuffisance professionnelle/faute simple*) are the reasons sought for dismissal. The interview must establish that the grounds are justified, and any outstanding holiday pay, the normal notice period and any other indemnities will not be effected.

In all *fautes* instances a first warning (*avertissement*) can be followed by a second warning (*blâme*) before leading to a 14-day suspension period. This procedure may be advisable, if it is felt that the fault was an isolated one, a result of extenuating circumstances, unlikely to be repeated, and that the employee deserves a second chance.

Whatever the circumstances, all employees leaving a company must be provided with:

- a *Certificat de Travail* which confirms the period of employment and the post occupied by the employee;
- a final payslip;
- and an *Attestation ASSEDIC* for the unemployment benefit authorities showing period employed, number of weekly hours, details of monthly salary over the preceding 12 months and final payment, including indemnities.

Employees are also entitled to a *Reçu pour solde de tout compte* which they must sign. This document confirms receipt of the *Certificat de Travail, Attestation ASSEDIC* and final pay slip and cheque for all outstanding salary and indemnities '*en paiement des salaires, accessoires du salaire, remboursements de frais et indemnities dus au titre de l'execution et de la cessation de mon contrat de travail*' or wording to that effect. The employee has up to two months to make any further payment claim after having received this *Reçu.*

Regrettably, redundancies may be the prelude to an unplanned sale of the business. How to sell a business is not the aim of this book, however, brief familiarity with the procedure below is important as it should be realised that redundancies can take time and will cost money:

- ◆ creditors, social security and tax offices should be informed and notified of the business' *avocat* or *notaire*;
- ◆ the final trading date should be established as well as the final set of accounts, clear of any debts;
- ◆ a copy of these accounts should then be sent to the tax office;
- ◆ once the tax office is satisfied that no further tax is due they will authorise your lawyer to release the sale proceeds which must be paid into the business' trading bank account which has been kept open for this very purpose.

USEFUL VOCABULARY

agent commercial	self-employed sales agent
agence d'intérim	temping agency
collaborateur	colleague
pavé publicitaire	display advertisement
petites annonces	classified advertisement
SMIC	national minimum salary
véhicule de fonction	vehicle for business use
VRP	salaried sales representative

Appendix 1

THE ADMINISTRATIVE *RÉGIONS* OF FRANCE AND THEIR *DÉPARTEMENT* DIVISIONS

Région	Département	Code no.
Alsace	Bas-Rhin	67
	Haut-Rhin	68
Aquitaine	Dordogne	24
	Gironde	33
	Landes	40
	Lot-et-Garonne	47
	Pyrénées-Atlantiques	64
Auvergne	Allier	03
	Cantal	15
	Haute-Loire	43
	Puy-de-Dôme	63
Basse-Normandie	Calvados	14
	Manche	50
	Orne	61
Bourgogne	Côte d'Or	21
	Nièvre	58
	Saône-et-Loire	71
	Yonne	89

Brétagne	Côte d'Armor	22
	Finistère	29
	Ille-et-Vilaine	35
	Morbihan	56
Centre-Val de Loire	Cher	18
	Eure-et-Loir	28
	Indre	36
	Indre-et-Loire	37
	Loir-et-Cher	41
	Loiret	45
Champagne-Ardenne	Ardennes	08
	Aube	10
	Marne	51
	Haute-Marne	52
Corse	Corse du Sud	2A
	Haute-Corse	2B
Franche-Comté	Doubs	25
	Haute-Saône	70
	Jura	39
	Territoire-de-Belfort	90
Haute-Normandie	Eure	27
	Seine-Maritime	76
Ile-de-France	Essonne	91
	Hauts-de-Seine	92
	Seine-et-Marne	77
	Seine-St.-Denis	93
	Val-de-Marne	94
	Val-d'Oise	95

	Ville de Paris	75
	Yvelines	78
Languedoc-Roussillon	Aude	11
	Gard	30
	Hérault	34
	Lozère	48
	Pyrénées Orientales	66
Limousin	Corrèze	19
	Creuse	23
	Haute-Vienne	87
Lorraine	Meurthe-et-Moselle	54
	Meuse	55
	Moselle	57
	Vosges	88
Midi-Pyrénées	Ariège	09
	Aveyron	12
	Gers	32
	Haute-Garonne	31
	Hautes-Pyrénées	65
	Lot	46
	Tarn	81
	Tarn-et-Garonne	82
Nord-Pas-de-Calais	Nord	59
	Pas-de-Calais	62
Pays de la Loire	Loire-Atlantique	44
	Maine-et-Loire	49
	Mayenne	53
	Sarthe	72
	Vendée	85

Picardie	Aisne	02
	Oise	60
	Somme	80
Poitou-Charentes	Charente	16
	Charente-Maritime	17
	Deux-Sèvres	79
	Vienne	86
Provence-Alpes-Côte-d'Azur	Alpes-de-Haute-Provence	04
	Alpes-Maritimes	06
	Bouches-du-Rhône	03
	Hautes-Alpes	05
	Var	83
	Vaucluse	84
Rhône-Alpes	Ain	01
	Ardêche	07
	Drôme	26
	Haute-Savoie	74
	Isère	38
	Loire	42
	Rhône	69
	Savoie	73

Appendix 2

SOME FALSE FRIENDS

French	Meaning	Possibly confused with
actuellement	at present, nowadays	actually
agenda	diary	agenda
blouse	overall, smock	blouse
brassière	baby's vest, life-jacket	brassiere
brasserie	pub	brassiere
cabinet	toilet, surgery, agency, office	cabinet
cachet	business/official stamp	something's prestigious quality
car	coach, bus, van	car
caution	guarantee, bail	caution
cave	cellar, wine retailer	cave
cellier	storeroom	cellar
chariot	shopping trolley	chariot
chips	potato crisps	chips
collège	secondary school	college
conducteur	driver, guide	conductor
conférence	lecture	conference
coordonnées	personal details (name, address...)	map coordinates
coordonnées bancaires	bank details (a/c number, etc.)	bank's situation

déception	disappointment	deception
désolé	sorry	desolate
diplôme	baccalauréat, further education diploma or higher education degree	college or university degree
éditer	to publish	to edit
evasion	excursion	evasion
éventuellement	possibly	eventually
formellement	positively, definitely	formally
herbe	grass	herb
ignorer	to not know, to be unaware of	to ignore
inhabité	uninhabited	inhabited
large	wide	large
libraire	book-seller	library or librarian
location	renting, reservation	location
mobile	portable house-phone	mobile phone
massif/ve	solid	massive
passer un examen	to take/sit an exam	to pass an exam
pétrôle	oil, petroleum	petrol
photographe	photographer	photograph
porc	pig, pigskin	pork
préservatif	contraceptive	preservative
professeur	teacher, master	professor
prune	plum	prune
radio	x-ray	radio
raisin	grape	raisin
réclamation	complaint	act of reclaiming
relation	relationship, acquaintance	relation

répertoire	index notebook, alphabetical list	repertoire
route	road	route
scotch	Sellotape	Scotch whisky
sensible	sensitive	sensible
spectacle	theatrical show, entertainment	spectacle
standing	luxury, de luxe (buildings)	standing (status/ position)
starter	car choke	starter (in car)
terrible	fantastic, great	terrible
veste	jacket	vest

Appendix 3

APPROXIMATE RESALE VALUES FOR BUSINESSES

The list below selects some businesses which may be of interest and particularly appropriate to foreigners.

The estimations drawn from Chamber of Commerce notes on national averages do not include the value of the premises themselves. The value of the business (*fonds de commerce*) is based on its commercial standing, patents, special permit and general goodwill on the one hand and its physical worth (*valeur corporel*) in terms of equipment, fittings and stock on the other. Some types of business, such as English bookshops or property surveillance, will only be relevant in certain localities. Others such as fast-food outlets and take away drinks stalls may be subject to a strong tourist-trade factor which is why the approximate values are based on daily takings.

Note the different values between similar, but not identical businesses, such as antique shops and second-hand goods, or cafés and brasseries with the latter serving meals as well as drinks. Additionally, the potential for the business, taking into account future developments in the area, will have a bearing. This long-term view should of course be taken before the creation of any new business.

Advertising agency (*agence de publicité*) 30 to 45% of turnover

Antiques shop (*antiquités*) 50 to 150% of turnover

Bazaar (*bazaar*) 25 to 50% of turnover

Bodywork shop (*carrosserie*) (garages 40 to 55% of turnover
selling new/second-hand cars and doing
mechanical repairs are not included here)

Brasserie 80 to 110% of turnover

Café 400 to 1,000 times
daily

takings

Cinema (independent) 30 to 75 times weekly
takings

Computer services (*informatique*) 25 to 50% of turnover

Dry-cleaners (*nettoyage à sec/pressing*) 70 to 110% of turnover

(English) bookshop (*librairie anglaise*) 45 to 60% of turnover
French *librairies*:

Estate agency (*agence immobilière*) Variable. Up to 5 times
average net profit

Fast-food 200 to 270 daily takings

Fishing tackle (*matériel de pêche*) 45 to 60% of turnover

Furniture store (*meubles – ventes*) 30 to 50% of turnover

General food store (*alimentation* 20 to 40% of turnover
générale)

Gift shop (*cadeaux*) 50 to 70% of turnover

Launderette (*laverie automatique*) 70 to 100% of turnover

Musical instrument shop 25 to 45% of turnover

Pet shop (*animalerie*) 40 to 45% of turnover

Plumbing, heating services (*plomberie,* 15 to 40% of turnover
chauffage)

Property management (*administrateur de bien*)	1.5 to 2.5 times management fees excl. VAT
Property surveillance (*gardiennage de biens*)	30 to 50% of turnover
Restaurant	60 to 120% of turnover
Removal company (*déménageur*)	30 to 70% of turnover
Second-hand goods (*brocante*)	40 to 75% of turnover
Mini-market (*superette*) (not to be confused with a supermarket (*supermarché*))	30 to 80% of daily takings
Take-away drinks stall (*buvette*)	40 to 100 times daily takings
Tourist hotel (*hotel de tourisme*)	Up to 3 times turnover
Travel agency (*agence de voyage*)	60 to 80% of commission generated
Tyre sales (*pneumatique vente*)	25 to 35% of turnover

These national average figures should serve only as a preliminary guide. They should be backed up by a consultation with the local Chamber of Commerce for a more precise estimation: either for a long-term appraisal of a new project or if the purchase of an existing business is being considered.

CHOOSING A FOREIGN EXCHANGE COMPANY? TRY CURRENCIES DIRECT

There has been a huge increase in the number of foreign exchange specialists who want to help you move your money to France. Deciding which one to use can be a daunting prospect but these simple guidelines should make the task a little easier.

◆ Select a company that has at least three years of audited accounts and is financially strong.

◆ Find out more information by doing a quick internet search on the company. Look out for whether they have won any awards or been recommended by a reliable source.

◆ Do not let a foreign exchange company pressurise you into doing a deal. Their job is to understand your requirements and to provide you with the information you need, not to hard sell and certainly not to make you trade until you are 100% happy.

◆ Ask what charges apply. If you are unsure, ask them to confirm in writing. You can really save money by using a well established, reputable foreign exchange company; not only through better rates but also as a result of lower transfer charges.

◆ Find out what foreign exchange buying options are offered. Some companies let you specify a rate at which you want to buy your currency (limit order) or fix a rate for up to 2 years (forward contract). These can be great tools to help you stick to your budget.

◆ Be aware that at present in the UK commercial foreign exchange is not an FSA regulated industry because it is not considered 'investment business'. Under the Money Laundering Regulations 2003, commercial foreign exchange companies are treated as "Money Service Businesses" which are covered by regulations administered by HM Customs & Excise.

Information provided by Currencies Direct.
www.currenciesdirect.com Tel: 0845 389 1729
Email: info@currenciesdirect.com

Index